PLANT-BASED DIET MADE SIMPLE

GARDEN of GRAPES.

First Edition: 2023

Published by Garden of Grapes.

Printed in USA

The recipes, techniques, and tips in this cookbook are intended for personal use only. The author and publisher are not responsible for any adverse effects or consequences resulting from the use of the recipes or suggestions in this book.

Library of Congress Cataloging-in-Publication Data:

First edition.
Includes index.

Manufactured in USA

Introduction

Ladies and Gentlemen,

Welcome, welcome, and thrice welcome to the "Plant-Based Diet Made Simple Cookbook." I invite you to embark on a culinary adventure like no other, as we dive headfirst into the vibrant world of plant-based cuisine. My name might not be as well-known as some, but let me assure you, my passion for food and flavor is as intense as any celebrity chef you might encounter.

Why a plant-based cookbook, you might wonder? The inspiration behind this venture is born from a deep love for delicious, wholesome food that fuels not only the body but also the soul. I've discovered, time and again, that a plant-based diet has the power to transform lives. It's more than a collection of recipes; it's a way of life.

Within these pages, you'll find a plethora of recipes that aren't just for those following a plant-based lifestyle but for anyone who craves simple, tasty, and nutritious meals. Whether you're a seasoned plant-based pro or a curious carnivore looking to expand your horizons, there's something here for you.

So, what can you expect from the "Plant-Based Diet Made Simple Cookbook"? Well, let me paint you a picture. Imagine page after page of mouthwatering, full-color photographs that will make your stomach rumble and your taste buds tingle. Visual feasts for the eyes that will inspire you to get into the kitchen and start cooking.

Now, think about simple yet exquisite recipes that require no culinary acrobatics or hours of your precious time. I know you're busy, and so am I. These recipes are designed with your everyday life in mind. Whether it's a quick breakfast, a satisfying lunch, or a cozy dinner with family and friends, these dishes are tailored for simplicity.

I've curated a diverse selection of recipes that showcase the endless possibilities of plant-based cooking. From hearty soups that warm your soul to zesty salads that dance on your palate, each recipe is a testament to the richness of flavors that Mother Earth provides. You'll find plant-based versions of classics, innovative creations, and international delights.

This cookbook isn't just about what you're eating; it's about how you're living. It's about embracing a diet that's gentle on the planet and kind to your health. It's about finding joy and satisfaction in the simplicity of real, unprocessed ingredients.

Now, as you delve into the pages that follow, I encourage you to savor the stories behind each recipe, the passion that goes into creating them, and the excitement of sharing them with you. Let this cookbook be a well-thumbed companion in your kitchen, a source of culinary inspiration, and a reminder that great food can be simple, healthy, and immensely satisfying.

So, without further ado, let's turn the page and start our journey together. I'm with you every step of the way.

Yours in flavor and simplicity,

Cooking Philosophy or Approach

Ladies and gentlemen, hungry souls, and fellow travelers on this culinary journey,

Allow me to invite you into the vibrant, mouthwatering world of the "Plant-Based Diet Made Simple Cookbook." When I set out on this gastronomic adventure, my aim was clear: to simplify the art of plant-based cooking and make it accessible to everyone. You see, in this cookbook, we have dispensed with complexity, shunned the unnecessary, and embraced a back-to-basics approach that celebrates simplicity and flavor in all their glory.

Food, at its essence, should not be daunting or esoteric. It should be a joyful and fulfilling experience, accessible to all. Our approach here is all about harnessing the natural vibrancy and goodness of plant-based ingredients. We champion the beauty of fresh produce and the culinary magic that can be conjured from a thoughtfully stocked pantry.

Technique-wise, we keep it straightforward. This cookbook is a celebration of the simple joy of cooking, but it's also an ode to the incredible diversity that plant-based foods offer. We'll explore techniques like sautéing, roasting, and grilling, and we'll master the art of crafting wholesome sauces and dressings. I've made sure that each recipe is not just a mere collection of ingredients and steps but a story, a narrative woven through the tactile sensations, rich flavors, and delightful aromas that permeate your kitchen.

Plant-based cooking is an invitation to experiment, to be adventurous, and to befriend a myriad of vegetables, legumes, grains, and spices that paint a vivid, nourishing tapestry. We will tread paths that span the globe, from hearty Mediterranean dishes to fragrant Asian inspirations, and you'll see that plant-based eating knows no bounds.

This cookbook is not about exclusion; it's about embracing the abundance that nature provides. It is an embodiment of the belief that plant-based cooking is a dynamic, flavorful, and absolutely satisfying way of life.

Here's a glimpse of the heart and soul of these recipes: we let the ingredients shine. It's about the sweetness of a perfectly roasted bell pepper, the creaminess of a ripe avocado, the earthy depth of a lentil, and the fragrant allure of fresh herbs. With the plant kingdom as our palette, we've created recipes that burst with color and vitality, recipes that will become cherished staples in your kitchen.

But let me be clear. The "Plant-Based Diet Made Simple Cookbook" isn't just about what you'll find on your plate. It's about the journey that brings you there. It's about the creative process, the act of cooking as a labor of love, and the ultimate satisfaction of savoring a meal that is as good for your body as it is for your taste buds.

So, fellow culinary adventurers, whether you're a seasoned plant-based pro or just dipping your toes into this world of vibrant flavors and healthful living, let this cookbook be your guide. It's an invitation to embrace the simplicity and beauty of plant-based cuisine, to revel in the flavors, and to embark on a journey toward a happier, healthier you.

Cook with joy, dine with delight, and savor each moment. Welcome to a world of flavor, to the "Plant-Based Diet Made Simple Cookbook."

Yours in the spirit of good food and good living,

Butternut Squash and Sage Risotto
See page, 31

Tips for Successful Cooking

Alright, my fellow home cooks, before we dive headfirst into the treasure trove of plant-based deliciousness within the pages of "Plant-Based Diet Made Simple," let's arm ourselves with some culinary wisdom. Cooking should be an enjoyable adventure, not a daunting task, and with a few tips and tricks, you'll be well on your way to becoming a plant-based culinary wizard.

1. Fresh is Best:
   When it comes to plant-based cuisine, freshness is the name of the game. Opt for fresh, seasonal produce whenever possible. They not only taste better but are also packed with more nutrients.

2. Knife Skills Matter:
   A good set of knives and some basic knife skills can make a world of difference. Practice your chopping, dicing, and mincing to speed up your prep time and ensure consistent cooking.

3. Embrace Herbs and Spices:
   Herbs and spices are the secret weapons in plant-based cooking. They add layers of flavor without the need for excessive fats or salts. Don't be afraid to experiment with different combinations.

4. Balance Your Plate:
   A well-balanced plant-based meal should include a variety of colors, textures, and nutrients. Aim for a mix of grains, legumes, vegetables, and fruits to ensure you're getting all the essential nutrients.

5. Properly Cook Grains and Legumes:
   Cooking grains like rice and quinoa, as well as legumes like beans and lentils, may require a bit of practice. Follow cooking instructions carefully, and remember that soaking certain legumes beforehand can reduce cooking time.

6. Roasting Magic:
   Roasting vegetables and tofu can transform them into flavor-packed delights. A little olive oil, your favorite seasonings, and a hot oven are your allies here.

7. Use Plant-Based Fats Wisely:
While many plant-based fats are healthy, they're calorie-dense. Use them sparingly, and consider options like avocados, nuts, and seeds for healthier fats.

8. Master the Art of Flavor-Building:
Building flavors takes time and patience. Start with a strong foundation—onions, garlic, and aromatics—and layer flavors as you go.

9. Be Mindful of Your Protein:
Plant-based protein sources include beans, lentils, tofu, tempeh, and seitan. Make them your friends and use them to add substance to your meals.

10. Taste as You Go:
Don't be afraid to taste and adjust as you cook. It's the mark of a great chef and ensures your dishes are seasoned to perfection.

Now that you're armed with these culinary insights, go forth with confidence, my friends. Whether you're a seasoned chef or a novice in the kitchen, the recipes in this cookbook are designed to be your guiding stars. Remember, there are no rules in cooking, only guidelines. Make each dish your own and let your taste buds be your compass.

Happy cooking, and here's to many plant-based culinary adventures!

Vegan Tikka Masala
See page, 37

Kitchen Essentials

Alright, my friends, let's talk kitchen essentials. You see, every artist has their tools, and in the culinary world, the kitchen is our canvas. So, whether you're a seasoned pro or just getting your feet wet in the plant-based game, these are the trusty sidekicks you'll want to have by your side as you embark on this flavorful journey.

1. Cutting Board: First off, a reliable cutting board is a must. Opt for a wooden or bamboo one; they're easier on your knives, and they don't harbor bacteria as much as the plastic varieties.

2. Sharp Knives: A good set of knives is the Jedi's lightsaber for a chef. Invest in a chef's knife, a paring knife, and a serrated knife. Keep them sharp – dull knives are dangerous and frustrating!

3. Measuring Cups and Spoons: When we're talking precision, you need measuring cups and spoons to get the right amount of ingredients for a perfect dish.

4. Food Processor/Blender: For the smoothest soups, sauces, and creamy creations, a trusty food processor or blender is a kitchen superstar. From silky cashew cream to luscious hummus, these tools are a must.

5. Cast Iron Skillet: There's something magical about a well-seasoned cast-iron skillet. It can take you from stovetop to oven and give your dishes that delicious sear.

6. Non-Stick Pan: For those quick sautés and stir-fries, a non-stick pan is your best friend. It helps you cook with less oil and avoids those dreaded stuck-on messes.

7. Oven and Baking Sheets: Every home chef needs an oven. And, don't forget the trusty baking sheets for those perfectly roasted veggies and more.

8. Cooking Pots and Pans: A variety of pots and pans in different sizes and materials is essential. Whether you're simmering a stew or whipping up a quick sauce, having the right cookware at your disposal is indispensable.

9.   Strainer/Colander: Sometimes, you need to give your ingredients a good rinse or drain. A sturdy strainer or colander does the job with ease.

10.   Mixing Bowls: Mixing up marinades, dressings, or simply tossing a salad, mixing bowls come in handy. Stainless steel or glass ones are excellent choices.

11.   Utensils: No chef can work without utensils. Make sure you have spatulas, tongs, a ladle, and a slotted spoon to help you work your culinary magic.

12.   Peeler and Grater: For those carrots, zucchinis, or citrus fruits, a peeler and a grater are indispensable.

13.   Storage Containers: Don't forget a stash of storage containers to keep your prepped ingredients or leftovers fresh and organized.

Now, here are some tips to keep in mind:

- Keep your knives sharp. Dull knives are not only frustrating but also dangerous.
- When measuring ingredients, do it right. Dry and liquid ingredients are measured differently.
- For easier clean-up, try to clean as you go. Trust me; it saves you a world of trouble later.
- Use appropriate cookware. A non-stick pan when you need one makes your life so much easier.
- Practice safe food handling. Always wash your hands and tools to prevent cross-contamination.
- Finally, embrace the joy of cooking. The best chefs have one secret ingredient: passion.

So there you have it, my friends. These are the essentials you'll want in your plant-based kitchen arsenal. With these trusty tools and a dash of enthusiasm, you'll be well on your way to creating delicious plant-based masterpieces.

Vegan Spanakopita
See page, 43

Flavor Pairing Suggestions

Alright, folks, here we are, at the heart of this culinary journey in the "Plant-Based Diet Made Simple Cookbook." We've taken you through a plethora of sumptuous plant-based recipes, ignited your taste buds, and hopefully, inspired some inner chefs.

But now, it's time to unleash your creativity in the kitchen. I'm not talking about a conventional cookbook's final chapter with a few recipes left for dessert. No, I'm talking about something that will set your culinary soul on fire - flavor pairing suggestions.

You see, great food isn't just about following recipes to the letter. It's about pushing the boundaries, experimenting, and creating something new and exciting right in your kitchen. The art of pairing flavors is where the magic happens, where ordinary dishes transform into extraordinary culinary experiences.

Here are some ideas for complementary flavors and ingredients that can work wonders together. But remember, these aren't strict rules; they're more like guiding stars in your culinary galaxy. Don't be afraid to twist and tweak, and always, always trust your taste buds.

1. Tomato + Basil + Garlic: This is a classic trio that Italians adore. The sweet acidity of tomatoes, the fresh aroma of basil, and the rich pungency of garlic. Perfect for pasta dishes, pizzas, and sauces.

2. Lemon + Dill + Cucumber: If you want a refreshing, zesty combination, this is it. Excellent for salads, dressings, and even chilled soups.

3. Cinnamon + Nutmeg + Cloves: When it comes to warm, comforting spices, this trifecta is a game-changer. It's fantastic for oatmeal, baked goods, and even savory dishes like curries.

4. Chili + Lime + Cilantro: For a spicy and tangy punch, you can't go wrong with these. Perfect for Mexican, Thai, or Indian cuisine.

5. Ginger + Soy Sauce + Garlic: If you're into Asian flavors, this trio is pure gold. It works wonders for stir-fries, marinades, and sauces.

6. Coconut + Curry Leaves + Mustard Seeds: An essential combination for South Indian cuisine, it delivers a rich, nutty flavor with a hint of earthiness.

7. Rosemary + Thyme + Sage: When you need your dishes to exude a hearty, herby aroma, this trio is your go-to. Great for roasts, stuffing, and potato dishes.

8. Chocolate + Vanilla + Sea Salt: For the sweet-toothed folks, this is heaven. The complexity of dark chocolate, the smoothness of vanilla, and the delightful contrast of sea salt. Works in both desserts and rich, savory dishes.

These suggestions are just the tip of the iceberg. Feel free to explore, mix and match, and create your own symphonies of flavor. Remember, it's about what makes your palate dance with joy.

So, in this chapter of flavor pairing suggestions, I'm not just giving you recipes; I'm giving you the keys to culinary creativity. Go ahead, unlock your inner chef, and let your kitchen be the canvas where you paint your flavor-filled masterpieces.

And please, never forget to have fun in the process. That, my friends, is what cooking is all about.

INDEX

Chapter 1
Sunrise Starters

2
pancakes

250

15

Vegan Banana Pancakes

Ingredients:

1 cup flour
2 tbsp sugar
1 tsp baking powder
1/2 tsp baking soda
1/4 tsp salt
1 cup almond milk
2 ripe bananas
1 tsp vanilla extract

Substitutions

None

Wake up with a smile! These fluffy pancakes are a vegan twist on a classic favorite.

Directions

1. Mash bananas in a bowl
2. In another bowl, mix dry ingredients
3. Combine wet and dry ingredients
4. Cook on a hot griddle
5. Serve with maple syrup

2
servings

180

10

Tofu Scramble

A protein-packed way to start your day. Tofu, veggies, and spices come together for a hearty breakfast.

Ingredients:

8 oz tofu
1/2 cup diced bell peppers
1/2 cup diced onions
1/2 cup spinach
1/2 tsp turmeric
1/2 tsp cumin
Salt and pepper to taste

Directions

1. Crumble tofu in a pan
2. Sauté veggies
3. Add spices
4. Cook until heated through
5. Season with salt and pepper
6. Serve hot

Substitutions

Substitute spinach with kale for variation

2 slices | 280 | 10

Avocado Toast with Chickpea Mash

Ingredients:

2 slices whole-grain bread
1 ripe avocado
1/2 cup cooked chickpeas
1 clove garlic
Juice of 1 lemon
Salt and pepper to taste

Substitutions

None

Creamy avocado meets zesty chickpea mash on crispy toast. A quick, nutritious morning treat.

Directions

1. Toast the bread
2. Mash avocado
3. Mash chickpeas with garlic and lemon juice
4. Spread on toast
5. Season with salt and pepper
6. Enjoy!

2
burritos

350

20

Vegan Breakfast Burritos

Ingredients:

4 large tortillas
8 oz tofu
1 cup black beans
1 cup diced bell peppers
1/2 cup diced onions
1 tsp chili powder
Salt and pepper to taste

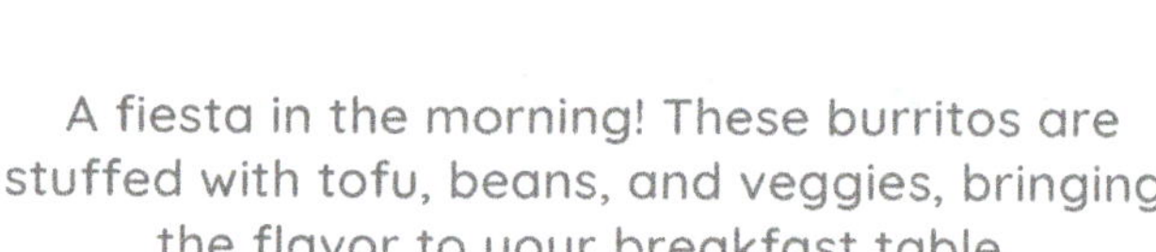

A fiesta in the morning! These burritos are stuffed with tofu, beans, and veggies, bringing the flavor to your breakfast table.

Directions

1. Crumble tofu in a pan
2. Add beans and veggies
3. Season with chili powder, salt, and pepper
4. Fill tortillas
5. Roll and serve hot

Substitutions

Substitute black beans with pinto beans if desired

2
servings

220

10

Blueberry Oatmeal

Ingredients:

1 cup rolled oats
2 cups almond milk
1 cup blueberries
2 tbsp maple syrup
1/2 tsp cinnamon
Pinch of salt

A comforting classic with a fruity twist. These blueberry oatmeal bowls will warm your heart and keep you full.

Directions

1. Combine oats and almond milk in a pot
2. Cook until creamy
3. Add blueberries, syrup, cinnamon, and salt
4. Stir well
5. Serve warm

Substitutions

Substitute blueberries with strawberries for a twist

2
servings

180

5

Chia Pudding with Berries

Ingredients:

1/4 cup chia seeds
1 cup almond milk
2 tbsp maple syrup
1/2 tsp vanilla extract
1 cup mixed berries
Fresh mint leaves for garnish

Overnight magic! Chia seeds turn into a creamy delight topped with vibrant berries.

Directions

1. Mix chia seeds, almond milk, syrup, and vanilla
2. Refrigerate overnight
3. Top with berries and mint
4. Enjoy!

Substitutions

None

2 slices   280   15

Vegan French Toast

Crispy outside, soft inside! Indulge in this vegan French toast made with a hint of cinnamon and a drizzle of syrup.

Ingredients:

4 slices whole-grain bread
1/2 cup almond milk
2 tbsp chickpea flour
1/2 tsp cinnamon
1/2 tsp vanilla extract
Maple syrup for serving

Directions

1. Whisk almond milk, chickpea flour, cinnamon, and vanilla
2. Dip bread slices
3. Cook until golden
4. Serve with maple syrup

Substitutions

None

2
servings

320

15

Breakfast Quinoa Bowl

Ingredients:

1 cup cooked quinoa
1 cup mixed berries
1/4 cup chopped nuts
2 tbsp maple syrup
1/2 tsp cinnamon
Pinch of salt

Protein-packed quinoa, fresh fruit, and nuts create a wholesome breakfast bowl to fuel your day.

Directions

1. Combine quinoa, berries, nuts, syrup, cinnamon, and salt
2. Mix well
3. Serve with a smile!

Substitutions

Substitute mixed berries with sliced peaches for a twist

2
servings

280

20

Sweet Potato and Black Bean Breakfast Hash

Hearty and flavorful! This hash combines sweet potatoes, black beans, and spices for a breakfast that sticks with you.

Ingredients:

2 cups diced sweet potatoes
1 cup black beans
1/2 cup diced onions
1/2 cup diced bell peppers
1 tsp paprika
Salt and pepper to taste

Directions

1. Sauté sweet potatoes, onions, and peppers
2. Add black beans and paprika
3. Season with salt and pepper
4. Cook until crispy
5. Serve hot

Substitutions

None

2
servings

200

10

Green Smoothie Bowl

A bowl of pure energy! Blend your greens, top with granola and fruit, and kickstart your day with a green smoothie bowl.

Ingredients:

2 cups spinach
1 ripe banana
1/2 cup almond milk
1/2 cup Greek yogurt
1 tbsp honey
1/2 cup granola
Sliced kiwi and strawberries

Directions

1. Blend spinach, banana, almond milk, yogurt, and honey
2. Pour into bowls
3. Top with granola and fruit
4. Enjoy your green goodness!

Substitutions

None

Chapter 2
Midday Feasts

2
sandwic
hes

300

15

Chickpea Salad Sandwich

Ingredients:

1 can chickpeas (drained and mashed)
1/4 cup diced celery
1/4 cup diced red onion
1/4 cup vegan mayo
1 tsp dijon mustard
Salt and pepper to taste

A protein-packed delight! This chickpea salad sandwich is perfect for a midday pick-me-up.

Directions

1. In a bowl, mix mashed chickpeas, celery, red onion, mayo, and mustard
2. Season with salt and pepper
3. Spread on bread
4. Assemble sandwiches
5. Enjoy!

Substitutions

None

2
servings

240

15

Vegan Caesar Salad

Ingredients:

4 cups Romaine lettuce
1/2 cup croutons
1/4 cup vegan Caesar dressing
1/4 cup cherry tomatoes
2 tbsp vegan parmesan
Lemon wedges for garnish

A plant-based twist on a classic. Creamy Caesar dressing over crisp lettuce with crunchy croutons.

Directions

1. Toss lettuce with dressing
2. Add croutons and cherry tomatoes
3. Sprinkle with vegan parmesan
4. Garnish with lemon
5. Serve with style

Substitutions

None

2
sandwic
hes

320

20

Vegan BLT Sandwich

Ingredients:

8 slices whole-grain bread
8 slices smoked tempeh
1 avocado (sliced)
2 lettuce leaves
2 tomato slices
Vegan mayo for spreading

Bites of perfection! A Vegan BLT with smoky tempeh, fresh tomatoes, crisp lettuce, and creamy avocado.

Directions

1. Pan-fry tempeh until crispy
2. Toast bread slices
3. Spread mayo on bread
4. Assemble sandwiches with tempeh, avocado, lettuce, and tomato
5. Serve with love

Substitutions

None

2
servings

280

20

Greek Quinoa Salad

Ingredients:

1 cup cooked quinoa
1 cup diced cucumbers
1/4 cup Kalamata olives
1/4 cup crumbled vegan feta
2 tbsp olive oil
Juice of 1 lemon
Oregano for garnish

A Mediterranean delight! Quinoa, cucumbers, olives, and feta cheese, all tossed in a zesty dressing.

Directions

1. Combine quinoa, cucumbers, olives, and feta in a bowl
2. Drizzle with olive oil and lemon juice
3. Sprinkle with oregano
4. Toss and serve

Substitutions

Substitute vegan feta with tofu feta for a twist

2
servings

350

20

Spicy Thai Noodle Salad

Ingredients:

6 oz rice noodles
1 cup shredded carrots
1/2 cup chopped bell peppers
1/4 cup chopped peanuts
2 tbsp peanut sauce
Fresh cilantro for garnish

A burst of flavors! Rice noodles, veggies, and a spicy peanut sauce make this Thai noodle salad irresistible.

Directions

1. Cook noodles according to package instructions
2. Toss with carrots, bell peppers, and peanuts
3. Drizzle with peanut sauce
4. Garnish with cilantro
5. Serve and savor

Substitutions

None

2 wraps | 260 | 10

Veggie Wrap with Hummus

Ingredients:

2 large whole-grain wraps
1/2 cup hummus
1/2 cup shredded carrots
1/2 cup sliced cucumber
1/2 cup baby spinach
Sliced red onion for flavor

Substitutions

None

A quick and nutritious wrap filled with colorful veggies and creamy hummus.

Directions

1. Lay out wraps and spread with hummus
2. Add carrots, cucumber, spinach, and red onion
3. Roll up tightly
4. Cut in half and serve
5. Enjoy!

2
servings

320

25

Vegan Buddha Bowl

Ingredients:

1 cup cooked brown rice
8 oz baked tofu
1 cup steamed broccoli
1/2 cup sliced bell peppers
1/2 cup shredded carrots
2 tbsp tahini dressing

A balanced bowl of goodness! Brown rice, tofu, and a rainbow of veggies, drizzled with tahini dressing.

Directions

1. Divide rice, tofu, broccoli, bell peppers, and carrots into bowls
2. Drizzle with tahini dressing
3. Enjoy your Buddha bowl!

Substitutions

None

2
servings

300

30

Roasted Vegetable and Quinoa Bowl

A bowl of roasted goodness! Colorful veggies and quinoa with a balsamic glaze.

Ingredients:

1 cup cooked quinoa
2 cups mixed roasted vegetables
2 tbsp balsamic glaze
Fresh basil leaves for garnish

Directions

1. Combine quinoa and roasted veggies in bowls
2. Drizzle with balsamic glaze
3. Garnish with fresh basil
4. Serve and savor

Substitutions

Substitute balsamic glaze with a lemon-tahini dressing for variety

2 rolls   280   30

Vegan Sushi Rolls

Ingredients:

4 sheets nori
1 cup cooked sushi rice
1/2 avocado (sliced)
1/2 cup sliced cucumber
1/2 cup shredded carrot
Soy sauce and wasabi for dipping

Sushi made simple! Roll up avocado, cucumber, and carrot in nori sheets for a delightful vegan sushi experience.

Directions

1. Place a bamboo sushi mat on a clean surface
2. Lay a nori sheet on the mat
3. Spread rice evenly on the nori
4. Add avocado, cucumber, and carrot
5. Roll tightly
6. Slice and serve with soy sauce and wasabi

Substitutions

None

2
servings

320

40

Vegan Stuffed Bell Peppers

Ingredients:

2 large bell peppers
1 cup cooked quinoa
1 cup black beans
1/2 cup diced tomatoes
1/2 cup diced onions
1/2 cup corn kernels
Tomato sauce for topping

Bell peppers filled with a savory mix of quinoa, black beans, and veggies, topped with tomato sauce.

Directions

1. Cut the tops off bell peppers and remove seeds
2. Mix quinoa, black beans, tomatoes, onions, and corn in a bowl
3. Stuff peppers with the mixture
4. Pour tomato sauce over
5. Bake until peppers are tender
6. Serve hot

Substitutions

Substitute black beans with lentils for variety

Chapter 3
Dinnertime Delights

4 servings **320** **30**

Vegan Chickpea Curry

Ingredients:

2 cups cooked chickpeas
1 onion (chopped)
2 cloves garlic (minced)
1 can diced tomatoes
1 can coconut milk
2 tbsp curry powder
Salt and pepper to taste

A hearty and flavorful curry with chickpeas, tomatoes, and spices, served over fragrant rice.

Directions

1. In a pot, sauté onions and garlic until fragrant
2. Add chickpeas, tomatoes, and coconut milk
3. Stir in curry powder, salt, and pepper
4. Simmer until thickened
5. Serve over rice
6. Enjoy!

Substitutions

None

4
servings

280

25

Mushroom and Spinach Stroganoff

Ingredients:

8 oz egg noodles
8 oz mushrooms (sliced)
2 cups baby spinach
1 onion (chopped)
2 cloves garlic (minced)
1 cup vegetable broth
1 cup vegan sour cream
Salt and pepper to taste

A creamy stroganoff made with tender mushrooms and spinach, served over egg noodles.

Directions

1. Cook noodles according to package instructions
2. In a pan, sauté mushrooms, onion, and garlic until browned
3. Add spinach and cook until wilted
4. Stir in broth and sour cream
5. Season with salt and pepper
6. Serve over noodles
7. Enjoy!

Substitutions

Substitute vegan sour cream with cashew cream for creaminess

4
servings

350

40

Vegan Lentil Shepherd's Pie

Ingredients:

2 cups cooked lentils
1 onion (chopped)
2 carrots (diced)
2 cloves garlic (minced)
1 cup frozen peas
1 cup vegetable broth
4 cups mashed potatoes
Salt and pepper to taste

Substitutions

None

Comfort food at its best! A hearty lentil filling topped with creamy mashed potatoes, baked to perfection.

Directions

1. Sauté onions, carrots, and garlic until softened
2. Add lentils, peas, and broth
3. Simmer until thickened
4. Season with salt and pepper
5. Spread mashed potatoes over the lentil mixture
6. Bake until golden
7. Serve hot
8. Enjoy!

4
servings

300

35

Vegan Thai Red Curry

Ingredients:

1 can coconut milk
2 tbsp red curry paste
8 oz tofu (cubed)
1 cup mixed vegetables
1 red bell pepper (sliced)
1 tbsp soy sauce
1 tsp sugar
Fresh basil leaves for garnish

Transport your taste buds to Thailand with this aromatic and spicy red curry packed with veggies and tofu.

Directions

1. In a pot, simmer coconut milk and red curry paste
2. Add tofu, vegetables, bell pepper, soy sauce, and sugar
3. Cook until veggies are tender
4. Garnish with basil
5. Serve with rice
6. Enjoy!

Substitutions

None

4
servings

320

30

Vegan Chili

Ingredients:

2 cans kidney beans
1 can diced tomatoes
1 onion (chopped)
2 cloves garlic (minced)
1 bell pepper (chopped)
2 tbsp chili powder
Salt and pepper to taste

Substitutions

Substitute kidney beans with black beans for
variation

A cozy bowl of chili filled with beans,
tomatoes, and spices, topped with vegan
cheese and avocado.

Directions

1. Sauté onions, garlic, and bell pepper until softened
2. Add beans, tomatoes, chili powder, salt, and pepper
3. Simmer until thickened
4. Top with vegan cheese and avocado
5. Serve hot
6. Enjoy your chili!

4
servings

350

40

Eggplant Parmesan

Ingredients:

2 large eggplants
2 cups marinara sauce
1 cup breadcrumbs
1 cup vegan mozzarella
1/2 cup vegan parmesan
Fresh basil leaves for garnish
Salt and pepper to taste

Substitutions

None

Layers of crispy eggplant slices, marinara sauce, and vegan cheese, baked to perfection.

Directions

1. Slice eggplants and season with salt
2. Dip in breadcrumbs
3. Bake until crispy
4. Layer with marinara sauce and vegan cheeses
5. Bake until bubbly
6. Garnish with basil
7. Serve hot
8. Enjoy your eggplant Parmesan!

4
servings

380

45

Vegan Jambalaya

Ingredients:

2 cups cooked rice
1 cup sliced vegan sausage
1 onion (chopped)
1 bell pepper (chopped)
2 cloves garlic (minced)
1 can diced tomatoes
1 tsp Cajun seasoning
Salt and pepper to taste

Substitutions

None

A taste of New Orleans! This vegan jambalaya is a spicy medley of rice, veggies, and vegan sausage.

Directions

1. Sauté onions, garlic, and bell pepper until softened
2. Add sausage and cook until browned
3. Stir in rice, tomatoes, Cajun seasoning, salt, and pepper
4. Simmer until heated through
5. Serve hot
6. Enjoy your jambalaya!

4
servings

340

40

Butternut Squash and Sage Risotto

Creamy risotto with roasted butternut squash, fresh sage, and a hint of nutmeg.

Ingredients:

2 cups Arborio rice
1 cup roasted butternut squash
2 tbsp olive oil
1 onion (chopped)
2 cloves garlic (minced)
4 cups vegetable broth
1/2 cup dry white wine
1/4 cup vegan parmesan
Fresh sage leaves for garnish
Salt and pepper to taste

Directions

1. Sauté onions and garlic in olive oil until translucent
2. Add rice and cook until lightly toasted
3. Stir in wine and cook until absorbed
4. Gradually add broth, one cup at a time, stirring until absorbed
5. Add butternut squash, parmesan, sage, nutmeg, salt, and pepper
6. Cook until creamy
7. Garnish with sage
8. Serve hot
9. Enjoy your risotto!

Substitutions

Substitute vegan parmesan with nutritional yeast for flavor

4 tacos | 280 | 30

Vegan Tacos with Black Beans

Ingredients:

8 small tortillas
2 cups cooked black beans
1 cup diced tomatoes
1/2 cup diced red onion
1/2 cup diced bell peppers
1 avocado (sliced)
1/4 cup chopped cilantro
1/4 cup vegan sour cream
Salt and pepper to taste

Substitutions

None

Taco night made vegan! Spicy black bean filling, fresh salsa, and creamy avocado in soft tortillas.

Directions

1. Warm tortillas in a pan
2. In a bowl, mix black beans, tomatoes, onion, and bell peppers
3. Fill tortillas with bean mixture, avocado, cilantro, and sour cream
4. Season with salt and pepper
5. Serve hot
6. Enjoy your vegan tacos!

4
sandwic
hes

320

30

Vegan BBQ Pulled Jackfruit Sandwiches

BBQ heaven! Pulled jackfruit smothered in barbecue sauce, piled high on buns with coleslaw.

Ingredients:

1 can young jackfruit (drained and shredded)
1 cup barbecue sauce
4 whole-grain buns
2 cups coleslaw
Salt and pepper to taste

Directions

1. In a pan, sauté shredded jackfruit until slightly browned
2. Stir in barbecue sauce, salt, and pepper
3. Cook until heated through
4. Assemble sandwiches with jackfruit and coleslaw
5. Serve hot
6. Enjoy your BBQ sandwich!

Substitutions

None

Chapter 4
Global Gastronomy

4
servings

320

30

Vegan Pad Thai

A taste of Thailand in every bite! This vegan Pad Thai combines rice noodles, tofu, and a tangy tamarind sauce.

Ingredients:

8 oz rice noodles
8 oz tofu (cubed)
1/4 cup tamarind paste
2 tbsp soy sauce
2 tbsp brown sugar
1 tsp chili flakes
1 cup bean sprouts
1/4 cup chopped peanuts
Fresh cilantro for garnish
Lime wedges for serving

Directions

1. Cook noodles according to package instructions
2. In a pan, sauté tofu until browned
3. Mix tamarind paste, soy sauce, brown sugar, and chili flakes
4. Add cooked noodles and sauce to the pan
5. Toss well
6. Serve with bean sprouts, peanuts, cilantro, and lime
7. Enjoy!

Substitutions

Substitute tofu with tempeh if desired

4
servings

300

40

Moroccan Chickpea Tagine

Ingredients:

2 cups cooked chickpeas
1 onion (chopped)
2 cloves garlic (minced)
1/2 cup dried apricots (chopped)
2 tsp Ras el Hanout spice blend
1/2 tsp ground cumin
1/2 tsp ground coriander
Salt and pepper to taste
Fresh cilantro for garnish

Substitutions

None

A fragrant and spiced Moroccan tagine with chickpeas, apricots, and a blend of North African spices.

Directions

1. Sauté onions and garlic in a tagine or large pot
2. Add chickpeas, apricots, and spices
3. Season with cumin, coriander, salt, and pepper
4. Simmer until flavors meld
5. Garnish with cilantro
6. Serve hot with couscous
7. Enjoy your Moroccan tagine!

4
servings

350

45

Vegan Tikka Masala

Ingredients:

8 oz tofu (cubed)
1 onion (chopped)
2 cloves garlic (minced)
1/2 cup tomato puree
1/2 cup coconut milk
2 tbsp vegan Tikka Masala paste
Salt and pepper to taste
Fresh cilantro for garnish

Creamy and rich Tikka Masala with marinated tofu, served with fragrant basmati rice and naan bread.

Directions

1. Marinate tofu in Tikka Masala paste
2. Sauté onions and garlic until softened
3. Add marinated tofu and cook until browned
4. Stir in tomato puree and coconut milk
5. Season with salt and pepper
6. Simmer until thickened
7. Garnish with cilantro
8. Serve with rice and naan
9. Enjoy!

Substitutions

Substitute tofu with seitan for a different texture

4
servings

280

45

Vegan Gyoza

Ingredients:

24 gyoza wrappers
8 oz tofu (crumbled)
1 cup chopped mushrooms
2 cloves garlic (minced)
1 tsp grated fresh ginger
2 tbsp soy sauce
1 tbsp sesame oil
1 tsp rice vinegar
Salt and pepper to taste
Green onions for garnish

Substitutions

None

Delicate Japanese dumplings filled with a savory mixture of tofu, mushrooms, and fresh ginger.

Directions

1. Combine tofu, mushrooms, garlic, ginger, soy sauce, sesame oil, rice vinegar, salt, and pepper in a bowl
2. Place a spoonful of the mixture in each gyoza wrapper
3. Fold and seal the edges of the wrappers
4. Steam or pan-fry until golden
5. Garnish with green onions
6. Serve with dipping sauce
7. Enjoy your vegan gyoza!

4
servings

320

40

Vegan Enchiladas

Layers of tortillas stuffed with a spicy black bean and vegetable mixture, smothered in enchilada sauce and vegan cheese.

Ingredients:

8 small tortillas
2 cups cooked black beans
1 cup diced tomatoes
1/2 cup diced onions
1/2 cup diced bell peppers
1 cup enchilada sauce
1 cup vegan cheese
Fresh cilantro for garnish

Directions

1. Mix black beans, tomatoes, onions, and bell peppers in a bowl
2. Fill tortillas with the mixture
3. Roll up and place seam-side down in a baking dish
4. Pour enchilada sauce over the tortillas
5. Sprinkle with vegan cheese
6. Bake until bubbly
7. Garnish with cilantro
8. Serve hot
9. Enjoy your vegan enchiladas!

Substitutions

None

4
servings

280

30

Vegan Ratatouille

Ingredients:

2 zucchinis (sliced)
2 eggplants (sliced)
2 bell peppers (sliced)
4 tomatoes (sliced)
1 onion (chopped)
2 cloves garlic (minced)
2 tbsp olive oil
1 tsp dried thyme
1 tsp dried rosemary
Salt and pepper to taste
Fresh basil for garnish

Substitutions

None

A colorful Provencal dish with layers of zucchini, eggplant, bell peppers, and tomatoes, seasoned with herbs.

Directions

1. Sauté onions and garlic in olive oil until softened
2. Arrange slices of zucchini, eggplant, bell peppers, and tomatoes in a baking dish
3. Drizzle with olive oil, thyme, rosemary, salt, and pepper
4. Cover with foil and bake until tender
5. Garnish with fresh basil
6. Serve hot
7. Enjoy your ratatouille!

4
servings

300

35

Ethiopian Lentil Stew

Ingredients:

1 cup red lentils
1 onion (chopped)
2 cloves garlic (minced)
2 tbsp berbere spice
1 cup diced tomatoes
4 cups vegetable broth
1/4 cup olive oil
Salt and pepper to taste
Injera bread for serving

A spicy and aromatic Ethiopian lentil stew with red lentils, berbere spice, and served with injera bread.

Directions

1. Sauté onions and garlic in olive oil until translucent
2. Add lentils and berbere spice, and cook for a minute
3. Stir in tomatoes, broth, salt, and pepper
4. Simmer until lentils are tender
5. Serve with injera bread
6. Enjoy your Ethiopian stew!

Substitutions

None

4
servings

350

45

Vegan Pho

Ingredients:

8 oz rice noodles
8 oz tofu (cubed)
1 onion (sliced)
2 cloves garlic (minced)
1 cinnamon stick
4 cups vegetable broth
2 tbsp soy sauce
Fresh basil and cilantro for garnish
Lime wedges for serving

Substitutions

None

A steaming bowl of Vietnamese pho with aromatic herbs, rice noodles, and tofu, served with lime and bean sprouts.

Directions

1. Cook rice noodles according to package instructions
2. In a pot, sauté onions and garlic until fragrant
3. Add cinnamon stick, broth, and soy sauce
4. Simmer until flavors meld
5. Remove the cinnamon stick
6. Serve hot with tofu, rice noodles, herbs, and lime
7. Enjoy your vegan pho!

4
servings

320

40

Vegan Spanakopita

Flaky and savory Greek spinach pie with a mixture of spinach, tofu, and herbs, wrapped in crispy phyllo dough.

Ingredients:

1 package phyllo dough
16 oz frozen spinach (thawed and drained)
8 oz tofu (crumbled)
1 onion (chopped)
2 cloves garlic (minced)
1/4 cup fresh dill
1/4 cup fresh parsley
1/4 cup olive oil
Salt and pepper to taste

Directions

1. Preheat oven to 350°F (175°C)
2. Sauté onions and garlic in olive oil until softened
3. Mix spinach, tofu, dill, parsley, salt, and pepper in a bowl
4. Brush phyllo sheets with olive oil and layer them
5. Add the spinach mixture
6. Fold and brush the top layer with oil
7. Bake until golden
8. Serve hot
9. Enjoy your vegan spanakopita!

Substitutions

None

4
servings

340

35

Vegan Bibimbap

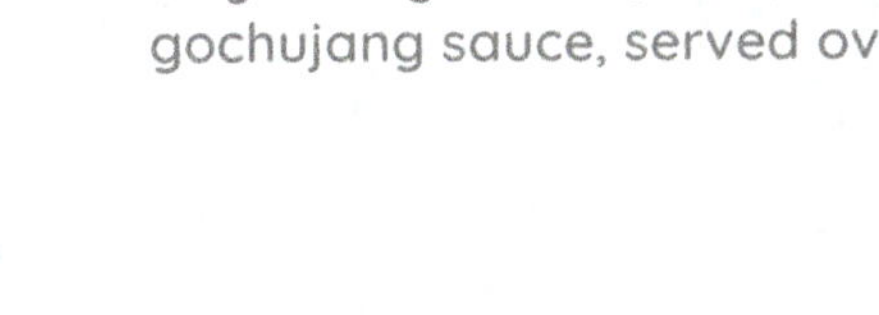

A Korean favorite! Bibimbap with a colorful array of vegetables, tofu, and a spicy gochujang sauce, served over rice.

Ingredients:

2 cups cooked rice
8 oz tofu (cubed)
1 cup sliced mushrooms
1 cup julienned carrots
1 cup spinach
4 cloves garlic (minced)
4 tbsp gochujang sauce
2 tbsp sesame oil
Salt and pepper to taste
Sesame seeds for garnish

Directions

1. Sauté tofu, mushrooms, carrots, and spinach until cooked
2. Mix garlic, gochujang sauce, sesame oil, salt, and pepper
3. Serve tofu and veggies over rice
4. Drizzle with sauce and garnish with sesame seeds
5. Enjoy your bibimbap!

Substitutions

None

Chapter 5
Pasta Pleasures

4
servings

320

30

Vegan Spaghetti Bolognese

Ingredients:

8 oz spaghetti
1 cup cooked brown lentils
1 onion (chopped)
2 cloves garlic (minced)
1 carrot (chopped)
1 celery stalk (chopped)
1 can crushed tomatoes
2 tsp dried oregano
Salt and pepper to taste
Fresh basil for garnish

Substitutions

None

A classic Italian favorite made vegan! Hearty tomato sauce with lentils and a medley of vegetables, served over spaghetti.

Directions

1. Cook spaghetti according to package instructions
2. Sauté onions, garlic, carrots, and celery until softened
3. Add lentils, tomatoes, oregano, salt, and pepper
4. Simmer until flavors meld
5. Serve sauce over spaghetti
6. Garnish with fresh basil
7. Enjoy your vegan Bolognese!

4
servings

350

25

Creamy Vegan Alfredo

Ingredients:

8 oz fettuccine pasta
1 cup cashews (soaked)
2 cloves garlic (minced)
1/4 cup nutritional yeast
2 cups almond milk
1/4 cup vegan butter
Salt and pepper to taste
Fresh parsley for garnish

Substitutions

None

Luxuriously creamy Alfredo sauce made with cashews and nutritional yeast, served over fettuccine pasta.

Directions

1. Cook pasta according to package instructions
2. Blend cashews, garlic, nutritional yeast, almond milk, and butter until smooth
3. Heat the sauce in a pan until thickened
4. Season with salt and pepper
5. Serve sauce over pasta
6. Garnish with fresh parsley
7. Enjoy your creamy Alfredo!

4
servings

320

20

Vegan Pesto Pasta

Ingredients:

8 oz pasta of your choice
2 cups fresh basil leaves
1/2 cup pine nuts
2 cloves garlic (minced)
1/2 cup olive oil
1/4 cup nutritional yeast
Salt and pepper to taste
Lemon juice for a zesty kick
Fresh basil for garnish

Substitutions

None

A burst of fresh basil and pine nuts in every bite! Vegan pesto sauce tossed with your favorite pasta.

Directions

1. Cook pasta according to package instructions
2. Blend basil, pine nuts, garlic, olive oil, nutritional yeast, salt, and pepper until smooth
3. Add lemon juice for extra flavor
4. Toss sauce with cooked pasta
5. Garnish with fresh basil
6. Enjoy your vegan pesto pasta!

4
servings

360

45

Vegan Lasagna

Layers of pasta, tofu ricotta, marinara sauce, and vegan cheese baked to perfection in this classic Italian dish.

Ingredients:

8 lasagna noodles (cooked)
2 cups marinara sauce
1 cup vegan mozzarella
1 cup tofu ricotta
1/4 cup vegan parmesan
Fresh basil leaves for garnish
Salt and pepper to taste

Directions

1. Preheat oven to 350°F (175°C)
2. Layer lasagna noodles with marinara sauce, tofu ricotta, and mozzarella
3. Repeat until all ingredients are used
4. Top with vegan parmesan
5. Bake until bubbly and golden
6. Garnish with fresh basil
7. Serve hot
8. Enjoy your vegan lasagna!

Substitutions

None

4
servings

340

30

Vegan Carbonara

A creamy and smoky carbonara sauce with tofu bacon, peas, and spaghetti, all veganized for your enjoyment.

Ingredients:

8 oz spaghetti
1 cup tofu bacon (chopped)
1 cup frozen peas
2 cloves garlic (minced)
1/2 cup almond milk
1/4 cup nutritional yeast
1/4 cup vegan parmesan
Salt and pepper to taste
Fresh parsley for garnish

Directions

1. Cook pasta according to package instructions
2. Sauté tofu bacon, garlic, and peas until heated through
3. Mix almond milk, nutritional yeast, vegan parmesan, salt, and pepper in a bowl
4. Toss sauce with cooked pasta
5. Serve hot
6. Garnish with fresh parsley
7. Enjoy your vegan carbonara!

Substitutions

None

4
servings

340

20

Spicy Peanut Noodles

Ingredients:

8 oz spaghetti
8 oz tofu (cubed)
1/2 cup peanut butter
1/4 cup soy sauce
2 tbsp rice vinegar
1 tbsp sriracha sauce
2 cloves garlic (minced)
1 cup mixed veggies
Salt and pepper to taste
Chopped peanuts for garnish

Substitutions

None

A symphony of flavors in every bite! Spaghetti noodles tossed in a spicy peanut sauce with veggies and tofu.

Directions

1. Cook pasta according to package instructions
2. Sauté tofu until browned
3. In a bowl, whisk peanut butter, soy sauce, rice vinegar, sriracha, and garlic
4. Toss sauce with cooked pasta, tofu, and veggies
5. Season with salt and pepper
6. Garnish with chopped peanuts
7. Enjoy your spicy peanut noodles!

4
servings

320

20

Vegan Mac and Cheese

Ingredients:

8 oz macaroni
1 cup cashews (soaked)
2 cups almond milk
1/4 cup nutritional yeast
1/4 cup vegan butter
1/2 tsp turmeric (for color)
Salt and pepper to taste
Chopped fresh chives for garnish

Creamy and dreamy vegan mac and cheese made with a velvety cashew-based sauce, perfect for indulging your comfort food cravings.

Directions

1. Cook macaroni according to package instructions
2. Blend cashews, almond milk, nutritional yeast, vegan butter, turmeric, salt, and pepper until smooth
3. Toss sauce with cooked macaroni
4. Garnish with fresh chives
5. Enjoy your vegan mac and cheese!

Substitutions

None

4
servings

300

25

Vegan Lemon Asparagus Pasta

A bright and zesty pasta dish with tender asparagus, lemon zest, and a touch of garlic, perfect for a light and flavorful meal.

Ingredients:

8 oz pasta of your choice
1 bunch asparagus (trimmed and cut into pieces)
2 cloves garlic (minced)
Zest of 1 lemon
Juice of 1 lemon
1/4 cup olive oil
Salt and pepper to taste
Fresh basil leaves for garnish

Directions

1. Cook pasta according to package instructions
2. In a pan, sauté asparagus and garlic until tender
3. Toss cooked pasta with asparagus, lemon zest, lemon juice, olive oil, salt, and pepper
4. Garnish with fresh basil
5. Enjoy your lemon asparagus pasta!

Substitutions

None

4
servings

350

35

Vegan Mushroom Risotto

Ingredients:

1 1/2 cups Arborio rice
8 oz mushrooms (sliced)
1 onion (chopped)
2 cloves garlic (minced)
4 cups vegetable broth
1/2 cup dry white wine
2 tbsp olive oil
Salt and pepper to taste
Fresh parsley for garnish

Substitutions

None

Creamy and earthy mushroom risotto cooked to perfection with Arborio rice, white wine, and vegetable broth.

Directions

1. Sauté onions and garlic in olive oil until translucent
2. Add mushrooms and cook until browned
3. Stir in rice and cook until lightly toasted
4. Pour in wine and cook until absorbed
5. Gradually add broth, one cup at a time, stirring until absorbed
6. Season with salt and pepper
7. Garnish with fresh parsley
8. Enjoy your mushroom risotto!

4
servings

280

20

Vegan Zucchini Noodles with Pesto

Ingredients:

4 medium zucchinis (spiralized into noodles)
1 cup cherry tomatoes (halved)
1/2 cup vegan pesto
Salt and pepper to taste
Fresh basil leaves for garnish

A light and refreshing dish with zucchini noodles, vegan pesto, and cherry tomatoes, perfect for a quick and healthy meal.

Directions

1. In a large bowl, toss zucchini noodles with cherry tomatoes
2. Add vegan pesto and mix well
3. Season with salt and pepper
4. Garnish with fresh basil
5. Enjoy your zucchini noodles with pesto!

Substitutions

None

We have a small favor to ask

My Fellow Culinary Adventurers,

As we delve into the heart of this culinary voyage, the "Plant-Based Diet Made Simple Cookbook," I want to take a moment to express my genuine appreciation for your companionship on this wholesome journey. We've embarked on a quest to simplify the art of plant-based cooking, and your presence here is a testament to your commitment to a healthier, more mindful way of life.

The creation of this cookbook was driven by a desire to make the transition to plant-based living as accessible and delectable as possible. The recipes within these pages are crafted with the utmost care and consideration for your well-being, as well as your taste buds.

Now, my friends, I must ask for your support. Reviews are the lifeblood of the culinary world, especially for small publishers like us. Your feedback provides guidance, inspiration, and motivation for the work we do, helping us refine our craft and navigate the ever-evolving landscape of plant-based cuisine.

Leaving a review is a small yet profoundly impactful gesture that can influence the choices and experiences of countless other culinary explorers. If the recipes you've encountered here have made your plant-based journey simpler, tastier, or more enjoyable, please consider taking a moment to leave a review.

A simple star rating and a few words of your thoughts on the platform or app where you obtained this cookbook would mean the world to us. Your review is a beacon that can light the path for others venturing into the world of plant-based living.

Every review, regardless of its length, resonates with us. We've put our hearts into this cookbook, and your feedback is a vital compass that keeps us on the right course. Even the most passionate culinary explorers can occasionally stumble, and your reviews help us identify and rectify those instances.

Now, as we continue to savor these delightful plant-based creations, I encourage you to reflect upon the many flavors, ingredients, and dishes that await you. We're about to embark on a culinary adventure like no other, and your valuable feedback will help shape the future of plant-based cuisine.

Thank you for being part of this culinary expedition, and I eagerly anticipate the exciting dishes we'll discover together. Your reviews are not only a boon to us but also a gift to your fellow culinary enthusiasts.

With heartfelt appreciation and the promise of more delectable discoveries,

Chapter 6
Comfort Creations

4
servings

320

40

Vegan Stuffed Peppers

Ingredients:

4 bell peppers (any color)
1 cup cooked brown rice
1 cup cooked brown lentils
1 onion (chopped)
2 cloves garlic (minced)
1 can diced tomatoes
1 tsp dried oregano
Salt and pepper to taste
Fresh parsley for garnish

Substitutions

None

A wholesome classic! Bell peppers stuffed with a flavorful mix of rice, lentils, tomatoes, and spices, then baked to perfection.

Directions

1. Preheat oven to 350°F (175°C)
2. Cut the tops off the peppers and remove seeds
3. Sauté onions and garlic until softened
4. Mix rice, lentils, diced tomatoes, oregano, salt, and pepper in a bowl
5. Stuff peppers with the mixture
6. Place in a baking dish and cover with foil
7. Bake until peppers are tender
8. Garnish with fresh parsley
9. Enjoy your vegan stuffed peppers!

4
servings

340

45

Vegan Meatloaf

A hearty meatloaf made with a savory mixture of lentils, mushrooms, and oats, smothered in a tangy tomato glaze.

Ingredients:

1 cup cooked brown lentils
8 oz mushrooms (chopped)
1 onion (chopped)
2 cloves garlic (minced)
1 cup rolled oats
1/4 cup tomato sauce
2 tbsp soy sauce
1 tsp dried thyme
Salt and pepper to taste

Directions

1. Preheat oven to 350°F (175°C)
2. Sauté mushrooms, onions, and garlic until softened
3. Blend lentils, mushroom mixture, oats, tomato sauce, soy sauce, thyme, salt, and pepper until combined
4. Press mixture into a loaf pan
5. Brush the top with extra tomato sauce
6. Bake until firm and browned
7. Slice and serve
8. Enjoy your vegan meatloaf!

Substitutions

None

4
servings

360

50

Vegan BBQ Ribs

Sticky and smoky BBQ ribs made with seitan, basted with a lip-smacking barbecue sauce for that perfect finger-licking experience.

Ingredients:

1 1/2 cups vital wheat gluten
2 tbsp nutritional yeast
2 tsp smoked paprika
1 tsp garlic powder
1/2 tsp onion powder
1 cup vegetable broth
1/4 cup barbecue sauce
2 tbsp soy sauce
Salt and pepper to taste

Directions

1. Preheat oven to 350°F (175°C)
2. Mix vital wheat gluten, nutritional yeast, smoked paprika, garlic powder, onion powder, salt, and pepper in a bowl
3. In a separate bowl, combine vegetable broth, barbecue sauce, and soy sauce
4. Pour wet ingredients into dry and knead until it forms a dough
5. Shape the dough into a rib-like form
6. Wrap in aluminum foil and bake for 30 minutes
7. Unwrap, brush with more barbecue sauce, and bake for an additional 10 minutes
8. Enjoy your vegan BBQ ribs!

Substitutions

None

4
servings

280

30

Vegan Buffalo Cauliflower Wings

Spicy and crispy cauliflower wings coated in tangy buffalo sauce, perfect for game day or any day you crave a little kick.

Ingredients:

1 head cauliflower (cut into florets)
1 cup flour
1 cup almond milk
1 tsp garlic powder
1 tsp onion powder
1/2 cup hot sauce
2 tbsp vegan butter
Salt and pepper to taste

Directions

1. Preheat oven to 450°F (230°C)
2. In a bowl, whisk flour, almond milk, garlic powder, onion powder, salt, and pepper until smooth
3. Dip cauliflower florets in the batter and place on a baking sheet
4. Bake until golden and crispy
5. In a saucepan, melt vegan butter and mix with hot sauce
6. Toss baked cauliflower in the buffalo sauce
7. Serve hot with your favorite dipping sauce
8. Enjoy your vegan buffalo cauliflower wings!

Substitutions

None

4
servings

320

25

Vegan Sloppy Joes

Ingredients:

1 cup brown lentils (cooked)
1 onion (chopped)
1 red bell pepper (chopped)
2 cloves garlic (minced)
1 can tomato sauce
2 tbsp tomato paste
2 tbsp maple syrup
1 tsp smoked paprika
Salt and pepper to taste

Substitutions

None

A messy delight! Lentil and vegetable filling simmered in a smoky and savory tomato sauce, served in buns for a comforting meal.

Directions

1. Sauté onions, bell pepper, and garlic until softened
2. Add lentils, tomato sauce, tomato paste, maple syrup, smoked paprika, salt, and pepper
3. Simmer until the sauce thickens
4. Serve in buns
5. Enjoy your vegan sloppy joes!

4
servings

300

20

Vegan Quesadillas

Ingredients:

8 small tortillas
2 cups cooked black beans
1 cup diced bell peppers
1 cup vegan cheese
2 tsp cumin
Salt and pepper to taste
Fresh cilantro for garnish

Substitutions

None

Cheesy and satisfying quesadillas stuffed with black beans, peppers, and vegan cheese, toasted to perfection.

Directions

1. Heat a tortilla in a pan
2. Sprinkle with vegan cheese, black beans, bell peppers, cumin, salt, pepper, and cilantro
3. Top with another tortilla
4. Cook until crispy and cheese is melted
5. Repeat for the remaining quesadillas
6. Slice and serve
7. Enjoy your vegan quesadillas!

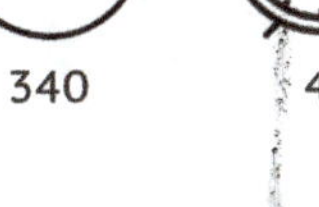

4
servings

340

40

Vegan Meatball Subs

Ingredients:

4 sub rolls
2 cups cooked black beans
1 cup rolled oats
1 onion (chopped)
2 cloves garlic (minced)
1 tsp dried basil
1 tsp dried oregano
1 cup marinara sauce
1 cup vegan mozzarella
Salt and pepper to taste
Fresh basil for garnish

Substitutions

None

Hearty vegan meatballs made with a blend of beans, oats, and spices, served in a sub with marinara sauce and vegan cheese.

Directions

1. Preheat oven to 350°F (175°C)
2. In a food processor, blend black beans, oats, onion, garlic, basil, oregano, salt, and pepper until combined
3. Form mixture into meatballs and bake for 20 minutes
4. Place meatballs in sub rolls, top with marinara sauce and vegan mozzarella
5. Bake until cheese is melted
6. Garnish with fresh basil
7. Enjoy your vegan meatball subs!

4
servings

360

35

Vegan Philly Cheesesteak

Ingredients:

4 hoagie rolls
2 cups seitan strips
1 onion (sliced)
2 bell peppers (sliced)
1 cup vegan cheese sauce
Salt and pepper to taste

A Philly classic gone vegan! Sautéed seitan strips, onions, and bell peppers smothered in vegan cheese and served in a hoagie roll.

Directions

1. Heat a pan and sauté seitan strips, onions, and bell peppers until softened
2. Add salt and pepper to taste
3. Fill hoagie rolls with the seitan mixture
4. Pour vegan cheese sauce on top
5. Serve hot
6. Enjoy your vegan Philly cheesesteak!

Substitutions

None

4
servings

320

30

Vegan Reuben Sandwiches

Ingredients:

8 slices rye bread
8 oz tempeh (sliced)
1 cup sauerkraut
1/2 cup vegan Swiss cheese
1/4 cup vegan Russian dressing
Olive oil for cooking
Salt and pepper to taste

Substitutions

None

A vegan twist on a classic Reuben sandwich with smoky tempeh, sauerkraut, vegan Swiss cheese, and Russian dressing.

Directions

1. Heat olive oil in a pan and sauté tempeh until browned
2. Season with salt and pepper
3. Toast rye bread slices
4. Spread Russian dressing on each slice
5. Layer tempeh, sauerkraut, and vegan Swiss cheese between slices
6. Grill until cheese is melted
7. Enjoy your vegan Reuben sandwiches!

Chapter 7
Fresh and Vibrant Salads

4
servings

350

20

Vegan Cobb Salad

A colorful medley of greens, avocado, chickpeas, tomatoes, and vegan bacon, drizzled with a creamy tahini dressing.

Ingredients:

8 cups mixed greens
1 cup cherry tomatoes (halved)
1 cup chickpeas (cooked)
1 avocado (sliced)
1/2 cup vegan bacon (crumbled)
1/4 cup red onion (chopped)
1/4 cup tahini
2 tbsp lemon juice
1 clove garlic (minced)
Salt and pepper to taste

Directions

1. In a large bowl, combine mixed greens, cherry tomatoes, chickpeas, avocado, vegan bacon, and red onion
2. In a separate bowl, whisk together tahini, lemon juice, garlic, salt, and pepper until smooth
3. Drizzle dressing over the salad
4. Toss to coat evenly
5. Serve and enjoy your vegan Cobb salad!

Substitutions

None

4
servings

280

15

Vegan Caprese Salad

Ingredients:

4 ripe tomatoes (sliced)
1 cup vegan mozzarella (sliced)
Fresh basil leaves
1/4 cup balsamic glaze
Salt and pepper to taste

A classic Caprese salad with a vegan twist! Fresh tomatoes, basil, and vegan mozzarella drizzled with balsamic glaze.

Directions

1. Arrange tomato slices and vegan mozzarella on a serving platter
2. Tuck fresh basil leaves between the slices
3. Drizzle with balsamic glaze
4. Season with salt and pepper
5. Enjoy your vegan Caprese salad!

Substitutions

None

4
servings

320

20

Vegan Waldorf Salad

Ingredients:

2 apples (diced)
1 cup celery (chopped)
1 cup red grapes (halved)
1/2 cup walnuts (chopped)
1/2 cup vegan mayonnaise
2 tbsp lemon juice
2 tbsp maple syrup
Salt and pepper to taste

Substitutions

None

A crunchy and sweet Waldorf salad with apples, celery, grapes, walnuts, and a creamy vegan dressing.

Directions

1. In a large bowl, combine diced apples, celery, grapes, and walnuts
2. In a separate bowl, whisk together vegan mayonnaise, lemon juice, maple syrup, salt, and pepper
3. Pour dressing over the salad
4. Toss to coat evenly
5. Serve and enjoy your vegan Waldorf salad!

4
servings

180

15

Vegan Watermelon Salad

A refreshing summer salad with juicy watermelon, cucumber, mint, and a zesty lime dressing, perfect for cooling down on hot days.

Ingredients:

4 cups cubed watermelon
1 cucumber (sliced)
1/4 cup fresh mint leaves
Zest and juice of 1 lime
1 tbsp agave syrup
Salt to taste

Directions

1. In a large bowl, combine cubed watermelon and cucumber slices
2. Sprinkle with fresh mint leaves
3. In a separate bowl, whisk together lime zest, lime juice, agave syrup, and salt
4. Drizzle dressing over the salad
5. Toss to coat evenly
6. Serve and enjoy your vegan watermelon salad!

Substitutions

None

4
servings

320

15

Vegan Caesar Salad

A classic Caesar salad with crunchy croutons, vegan Caesar dressing, and a sprinkle of vegan parmesan cheese.

Ingredients:

8 cups romaine lettuce (chopped)
1 cup croutons
1/4 cup vegan Caesar dressing
1/4 cup vegan parmesan
Lemon wedges for garnish

Directions

1. In a large bowl, combine chopped romaine lettuce and croutons
2. Drizzle with vegan Caesar dressing and toss to coat evenly
3. Sprinkle with vegan parmesan cheese
4. Garnish with lemon wedges
5. Enjoy your vegan Caesar salad!

Substitutions

None

4
servings

280

15

Vegan Greek Salad

Ingredients:

4 cups cucumber (sliced)
2 cups cherry tomatoes (halved)
1/2 cup Kalamata olives (pitted)
1/4 cup red onion (thinly sliced)
1/2 cup vegan feta cheese (cubed)
1/4 cup Greek dressing
Salt and pepper to taste

A Mediterranean delight! Crisp cucumbers, juicy tomatoes, olives, red onion, and vegan feta cheese tossed in Greek dressing.

Directions

1. In a large bowl, combine sliced cucumbers, cherry tomatoes, Kalamata olives, red onion, and vegan feta cheese
2. Drizzle with Greek dressing
3. Season with salt and pepper
4. Toss to coat evenly
5. Enjoy your vegan Greek salad!

Substitutions

None

4
servings

320

20

Vegan Southwestern Salad

Ingredients:

8 cups mixed greens
1 cup black beans (cooked)
1 cup corn (cooked)
1 red bell pepper (chopped)
1 avocado (sliced)
1/4 cup fresh cilantro (chopped)
Zest and juice of 1 lime
2 tbsp olive oil
Salt and pepper to taste

Substitutions

None

A vibrant Southwestern salad with black beans, corn, bell peppers, avocado, and a zesty lime-cilantro dressing.

Directions

1. In a large bowl, combine mixed greens, black beans, corn, red bell pepper, and avocado
2. In a separate bowl, whisk together lime zest, lime juice, olive oil, salt, and pepper
3. Drizzle dressing over the salad
4. Sprinkle with fresh cilantro
5. Toss to coat evenly
6. Serve and enjoy your vegan Southwestern salad!

4
servings

280

20

Vegan Asian Slaw

A crunchy and colorful Asian slaw with cabbage, carrots, bell peppers, and a sesame ginger dressing.

Ingredients:

6 cups shredded cabbage
1 cup shredded carrots
1 red bell pepper (thinly sliced)
1/4 cup green onions (chopped)
1/4 cup sesame ginger dressing
2 tbsp sesame seeds
Salt and pepper to taste

Directions

1. In a large bowl, combine shredded cabbage, shredded carrots, red bell pepper, and green onions
2. Drizzle with sesame ginger dressing
3. Sprinkle with sesame seeds, salt, and pepper
4. Toss to coat evenly
5. Serve and enjoy your vegan Asian slaw!

Substitutions

None

4
servings

240

20

Vegan Broccoli Salad

Ingredients:

6 cups broccoli florets
1/2 cup raisins
1/4 cup sunflower seeds
1/2 cup vegan mayonnaise
2 tbsp apple cider vinegar
2 tbsp maple syrup
Salt and pepper to taste

A creamy and crunchy broccoli salad with raisins, sunflower seeds, and a tangy vegan dressing.

Directions

1. In a large bowl, combine broccoli florets, raisins, and sunflower seeds
2. In a separate bowl, whisk together vegan mayonnaise, apple cider vinegar, maple syrup, salt, and pepper
3. Drizzle dressing over the salad
4. Toss to coat evenly
5. Serve and enjoy your vegan broccoli salad!

Substitutions

None

4
servings

320

20

Vegan Kale Salad with Lemon Tahini Dressing

A nutrient-packed kale salad with chickpeas, cherry tomatoes, and a zesty lemon tahini dressing, perfect for a healthy meal.

Ingredients:

8 cups kale leaves (chopped)
1 cup cherry tomatoes (halved)
1 cup chickpeas (cooked)
1/4 cup tahini
2 tbsp lemon juice
1 clove garlic (minced)
2 tsp maple syrup
Salt and pepper to taste

Directions

1. In a large bowl, combine chopped kale leaves, cherry tomatoes, and chickpeas
2. In a separate bowl, whisk together tahini, lemon juice, garlic, maple syrup, salt, and pepper
3. Drizzle dressing over the salad
4. Toss to coat evenly
5. Serve and enjoy your vegan kale salad with lemon tahini dressing!

Substitutions

None

Chapter 8
Savory Soups and Stews

6
servings

220

30

Vegan Minestrone Soup

A hearty Italian classic! A medley of vegetables, beans, pasta, and herbs in a flavorful tomato-based broth.

Ingredients:

1 onion (chopped)
2 cloves garlic (minced)
2 carrots (sliced)
2 celery stalks (sliced)
1 zucchini (diced)
1 cup green beans (cut into pieces)
1 can diced tomatoes
1 can kidney beans (drained and rinsed)
6 cups vegetable broth
1 cup small pasta
1 tsp dried basil
1 tsp dried oregano
Salt and pepper to taste

Directions

1. In a large pot, sauté onions and garlic until fragrant
2. Add carrots, celery, zucchini, and green beans
3. Stir in diced tomatoes, kidney beans, vegetable broth, pasta, basil, oregano, salt, and pepper
4. Bring to a boil, then reduce heat and simmer for 15-20 minutes, or until pasta is tender
5. Serve hot and enjoy your vegan Minestrone soup!

Substitutions

None

4
servings

180

25

Vegan Tomato Basil Soup

A classic tomato soup with a vegan twist! Rich and velvety, with fresh basil for a burst of flavor.

Ingredients:

1 onion (chopped)
2 cloves garlic (minced)
2 cans diced tomatoès
1 can tomato sauce
1/4 cup fresh basil leaves
2 cups vegetable broth
1/2 cup coconut milk
Salt and pepper to taste

Directions

1. In a large pot, sauté onions and garlic until softened
2. Add diced tomatoes, tomato sauce, and vegetable broth
3. Simmer for 15-20 minutes
4. Blend soup until smooth using an immersion blender
5. Stir in coconut milk, salt, and pepper
6. Garnish with fresh basil leaves
7. Enjoy your vegan tomato basil soup!

Substitutions

None

4
servings

250

30

Vegan Potato Leek Soup

Ingredients:

2 leeks (sliced)
4 potatoes (peeled and diced)
4 cups vegetable broth
1 cup almond milk
1 tsp dried thyme
Salt and pepper to taste

Substitutions

None

Creamy and comforting potato leek soup made with tender potatoes, leeks, and a hint of thyme.

Directions

1. In a large pot, sauté leeks until softened
2. Add diced potatoes, vegetable broth, almond milk, thyme, salt, and pepper
3. Simmer until potatoes are tender
4. Use an immersion blender to blend soup until smooth
5. Serve hot and enjoy your vegan potato leek soup!

6
servings

280

30

Vegan Lentil Soup

A nutritious and satisfying lentil soup with vegetables, herbs, and a touch of lemon for brightness.

Ingredients:

1 onion (chopped)
2 cloves garlic (minced)
1 cup dried green or brown lentils
2 carrots (sliced)
2 celery stalks (sliced)
1 can diced tomatoes
6 cups vegetable broth
1 tsp dried thyme
Zest and juice of 1 lemon
Salt and pepper to taste

Directions

1. In a large pot, sauté onions and garlic until fragrant
2. Add lentils, carrots, celery, diced tomatoes, vegetable broth, thyme, salt, and pepper
3. Bring to a boil, then reduce heat and simmer for 20-25 minutes, or until lentils are tender
4. Stir in lemon zest and juice
5. Serve hot and enjoy your vegan lentil soup!

Substitutions

None

4
servings

220

35

Vegan Butternut Squash Soup

Ingredients:

1 butternut squash (peeled, seeded, and diced)
1 onion (chopped)
2 cloves garlic (minced)
4 cups vegetable broth
1/2 cup coconut milk
1/4 cup maple syrup
1/4 tsp ground nutmeg
Salt and pepper to taste

Substitutions

None

Creamy and velvety butternut squash soup with a hint of warmth from nutmeg and a touch of sweetness from maple syrup.

Directions

1. In a large pot, sauté onions and garlic until softened
2. Add diced butternut squash, vegetable broth, coconut milk, maple syrup, nutmeg, salt, and pepper
3. Simmer for 20-25 minutes, or until squash is tender
4. Use an immersion blender to blend soup until smooth
5. Serve hot and enjoy your vegan butternut squash soup!

6
servings

320

40

Vegan Gumbo

A spicy and flavorful vegan gumbo with okra, bell peppers, tomatoes, and a rich roux, served over rice.

Ingredients:

1 onion (chopped)
2 cloves garlic (minced)
2 bell peppers (chopped)
1 cup okra (sliced)
1 can diced tomatoes
1 cup vegetable broth
1 cup okra (sliced)
1 can diced tomatoes
1 cup vegetable broth
2 tsp Cajun seasoning
2 tbsp flour
2 tbsp vegetable oil
Cooked rice for serving
Salt and pepper to taste

Directions

1. In a large pot, heat vegetable oil over medium heat
2. Stir in flour to make a roux and cook until dark brown, stirring constantly
3. Add onions, garlic, bell peppers, and okra
4. Sauté until vegetables are softened
5. Add diced tomatoes, vegetable broth, Cajun seasoning, salt, and pepper
6. Simmer for 20-25 minutes
7. Serve hot over cooked rice
8. Enjoy your vegan gumbo!

Substitutions

None

4
servings

210

30

Vegan Mushroom Soup

A creamy and earthy mushroom soup with sautéed mushrooms, onions, and a hint of thyme, perfect for mushroom lovers.

Ingredients:

8 oz mushrooms (sliced)
1 onion (chopped)
2 cloves garlic (minced)
4 cups vegetable broth
1 cup almond milk
1 tsp dried thyme
Salt and pepper to taste

Directions

1. In a large pot, sauté mushrooms, onions, and garlic until mushrooms are browned
2. Add vegetable broth, almond milk, thyme, salt, and pepper
3. Simmer for 15-20 minutes
4. Use an immersion blender to blend soup until smooth
5. Serve hot and enjoy your vegan mushroom soup!

Substitutions

None

4
servings

280

30

Vegan Thai Coconut Soup

Ingredients:

2 cans coconut milk
4 cups vegetable broth
2 stalks lemongrass (sliced)
1 thumb-sized piece of ginger (sliced)
4 cloves garlic (minced)
2 cups mixed mushrooms
1 block tofu (cubed)
2 tbsp soy sauce
Zest and juice of 2 limes
Fresh cilantro for garnish
Salt and pepper to taste

Substitutions

None

A fragrant and creamy Thai coconut soup with lemongrass, ginger, and a burst of citrus from lime juice.

Directions

1. In a large pot, combine coconut milk, vegetable broth, lemongrass, ginger, and garlic
2. Bring to a simmer and cook for 15-20 minutes
3. Remove lemongrass and ginger
4. Stir in mushrooms, tofu, soy sauce, lime zest, and lime juice
5. Simmer until mushrooms are tender
6. Season with salt and pepper
7. Garnish with fresh cilantro
8. Enjoy your vegan Thai coconut soup!

4
servings

250

30

Vegan Black Bean Soup

A hearty and wholesome black bean soup with bell peppers, tomatoes, and a blend of spices for a zesty kick.

Ingredients:

2 cans black beans (drained and rinsed)
1 onion (chopped)
2 cloves garlic (minced)
2 bell peppers (chopped)
1 can diced tomatoes
4 cups vegetable broth
2 tsp cumin
1 tsp chili powder
1 tsp paprika
Salt and pepper to taste

Directions

1. In a large pot, sauté onions and garlic until softened
2. Add bell peppers, black beans, diced tomatoes, vegetable broth, cumin, chili powder, paprika, salt, and pepper
3. Simmer for 20-25 minutes
4. Use an immersion blender to blend soup until partially smooth, leaving some chunks
5. Serve hot and enjoy your vegan black bean soup!

Substitutions

None

4
servings

220

40

Vegan Split Pea Soup

Ingredients:

2 cups dried split peas
1 onion (chopped)
2 carrots (sliced)
2 celery stalks (sliced)
2 cloves garlic (minced)
6 cups vegetable broth
1 tsp dried thyme
Salt and pepper to taste

Substitutions

None

A comforting split pea soup with tender peas, carrots, celery, and a touch of thyme for a classic flavor.

Directions

1. In a large pot, combine split peas, onions, carrots, celery, garlic, vegetable broth, thyme, salt, and pepper
2. Bring to a boil, then reduce heat and simmer for 30-35 minutes, or until peas are tender
3. Use an immersion blender to blend soup until smooth
4. Serve hot and enjoy your vegan split pea soup!

Chapter 9
One-Pot Wonders

4
servings

380

45

Vegan Paella

A flavorful Spanish classic! A medley of saffron-infused rice, vegetables, and tender tofu, cooked to perfection.

Ingredients:

1 onion (chopped)
2 cloves garlic (minced)
1 red bell pepper (sliced)
1 yellow bell pepper (sliced)
1 cup Arborio rice
1 tsp smoked paprika
A pinch of saffron threads (dissolved in hot water)
2 cups vegetable broth
1 cup frozen peas
1 cup artichoke hearts (quartered)
8 oz firm tofu (cubed)
Salt and pepper to taste
Lemon wedges for garnish

Substitutions

None

Directions

1. In a large skillet, sauté onions and garlic until softened
2. Add sliced bell peppers and cook until tender
3. Stir in Arborio rice and smoked paprika
4. Pour in saffron-infused water and vegetable broth
5. Add frozen peas and artichoke hearts
6. Place cubed tofu on top
7. Cover and simmer for 20-25 minutes, or until rice is cooked and liquid is absorbed
8. Season with salt and pepper
9. Garnish with lemon wedges
10. Enjoy your vegan paella!

6
servings

320

30

Vegan Quinoa Chili

A hearty and protein-packed chili made with quinoa, beans, tomatoes, and a blend of spices for a kick of flavor.

Ingredients:

1 onion (chopped)
2 cloves garlic (minced)
1 red bell pepper (chopped)
1 green bell pepper (chopped)
1 cup quinoa
1 can black beans (drained and rinsed)
1 can kidney beans (drained and rinsed)
1 can diced tomatoes
4 cups vegetable broth
2 tsp chili powder
1 tsp cumin
1 tsp paprika
Salt and pepper to taste

Directions

1. In a large pot, sauté onions and garlic until fragrant
2. Add chopped bell peppers and cook until softened
3. Stir in quinoa, black beans, kidney beans, diced tomatoes, vegetable broth, chili powder, cumin, paprika, salt, and pepper
4. Simmer for 20-25 minutes, or until quinoa is cooked and chili thickens
5. Serve hot and enjoy your vegan quinoa chili!

Substitutions

None

4 servings

200

35

Vegan Ratatouille

A colorful and comforting French classic! Layers of thinly sliced vegetables baked in a tomato sauce with herbs.

Ingredients:

1 eggplant (sliced)
2 zucchinis (sliced)
2 tomatoes (sliced)
1 onion (sliced)
2 cloves garlic (minced)
1 can diced tomatoes
2 tbsp olive oil
1 tsp dried thyme
1 tsp dried basil
Salt and pepper to taste
Fresh basil leaves for garnish

Directions

1. Preheat oven to 375°F (190°C)
2. In a baking dish, layer sliced eggplant, zucchinis, tomatoes, onion, and minced garlic
3. Pour canned diced tomatoes over the vegetables
4. Drizzle with olive oil and sprinkle with dried thyme, dried basil, salt, and pepper
5. Cover with aluminum foil and bake for 30 minutes
6. Remove foil and bake for an additional 20-25 minutes, or until vegetables are tender and slightly browned
7. Garnish with fresh basil leaves
8. Enjoy your vegan ratatouille!

Substitutions

None

4
servings

280

35

Vegan Sweet Potato Curry

Ingredients:

2 sweet potatoes (peeled and cubed)
1 onion (chopped)
2 cloves garlic (minced)
1 can chickpeas (drained and rinsed)
2 cups spinach
1 can coconut milk
2 tbsp red curry paste
2 tbsp olive oil
2 cups cooked rice
Salt and pepper to taste

Substitutions

None

A creamy and fragrant curry with sweet potatoes, chickpeas, and spinach, served over rice for a satisfying meal.

Directions

1. In a large skillet, heat olive oil and sauté onions and garlic until softened
2. Add cubed sweet potatoes and cook until slightly browned
3. Stir in chickpeas, red curry paste, and coconut milk
4. Simmer for 15-20 minutes, or until sweet potatoes are tender
5. Add spinach and cook until wilted
6. Season with salt and pepper
7. Serve hot over cooked rice
8. Enjoy your vegan sweet potato curry!

4
servings

300

30

Vegan Teriyaki Stir-Fry

A quick and flavorful stir-fry with tofu, broccoli, bell peppers, and a homemade teriyaki sauce.

Ingredients:

8 oz tofu (cubed)
2 cups broccoli florets
2 bell peppers (sliced)
1 onion (sliced)
1/2 cup teriyaki sauce (see recipe below)
2 cups cooked brown rice
2 tbsp vegetable oil
Salt and pepper to taste

Directions

Teriyaki Sauce Ingredients:
1/4 cup soy sauce
1/4 cup water
2 tbsp maple syrup
2 cloves garlic (minced)
1 tsp ginger (minced)
1 tbsp cornstarch (dissolved in 2 tbsp water)

Substitutions

1. In a large skillet, heat vegetable oil and sauté tofu until browned
2. Add broccoli, bell peppers, and onions
3. Stir in teriyaki sauce and cook until vegetables are tender
4. Season with salt and pepper
5. Serve hot over cooked brown rice
6. Enjoy your vegan teriyaki stir-fry!

4
servings

320

40

Vegan Lemon Herb Risotto

Ingredients:

1 cup Arborio rice
1 onion (chopped)
2 cloves garlic (minced)
4 cups vegetable broth
1/2 cup white wine (optional)
Zest and juice of 2 lemons
2 tbsp fresh basil (chopped)
2 tbsp fresh parsley (chopped)
2 tbsp vegan butter
Salt and pepper to taste

Substitutions

None

A creamy and aromatic risotto infused with lemon and fresh herbs, perfect for a special meal.

Directions

1. In a large pot, sauté onions and garlic until softened
2. Add Arborio rice and cook for 2-3 minutes until translucent
3. If using, pour in white wine and stir until absorbed
4. Gradually add vegetable broth, one ladle at a time, stirring until absorbed before adding more
5. Continue this process until rice is creamy and tender (about 20-25 minutes)
6. Stir in lemon zest, lemon juice, fresh basil, fresh parsley, vegan butter, salt, and pepper
7. Serve hot and enjoy your vegan lemon herb risotto!

4
servings

250

25

Vegan Mexican Rice

A flavorful and colorful Mexican rice dish with tomatoes, bell peppers, and a blend of spices.

Ingredients:

1 cup long-grain white rice
1 onion (chopped)
1 red bell pepper (chopped)
1 green bell pepper (chopped)
1 can diced tomatoes
2 cups vegetable broth
2 tsp chili powder
1 tsp cumin
1 tsp paprika
Salt and pepper to taste

Directions

1. In a large skillet, sauté onions until translucent
2. Add rice and cook until lightly browned
3. Stir in chopped bell peppers, diced tomatoes, vegetable broth, chili powder, cumin, paprika, salt, and pepper
4. Bring to a boil, then reduce heat to low
5. Cover and simmer for 15-20 minutes, or until rice is cooked and liquid is absorbed
6. Fluff with a fork and serve hot
7. Enjoy your vegan Mexican rice!

Substitutions

None

4
servings

220

30

Vegan Cauliflower Fried Rice

Ingredients:

1 head cauliflower (grated into "rice")
8 oz tofu (cubed)
1 cup frozen peas and carrots
2 cloves garlic (minced)
2 tbsp soy sauce
1 tbsp sesame oil
1 tsp ginger (minced)
2 green onions (chopped)
Salt and pepper to taste

Substitutions

None

A low-carb twist on fried rice! Cauliflower rice stir-fried with vegetables and tofu in a savory sauce.

Directions

1. In a large skillet, sauté tofu until browned
2. Add minced garlic and grated cauliflower
3. Stir in frozen peas and carrots, soy sauce, sesame oil, ginger, salt, and pepper
4. Cook until cauliflower is tender and everything is well combined
5. Garnish with chopped green onions
6. Serve hot and enjoy your vegan cauliflower fried rice!

4
servings

280

30

Vegan Chickpea and Spinach Curry

A quick and nutritious curry with chickpeas, spinach, and a blend of aromatic spices, served over rice or naan.

Ingredients:

2 cans chickpeas (drained and rinsed)
1 onion (chopped)
2 cloves garlic (minced)
2 cups spinach
1 can coconut milk
2 tbsp curry powder
1 tsp cumin
1 tsp paprika
2 tbsp vegetable oil
Salt and pepper to taste
Cooked rice or naan for serving

Directions

1. In a large skillet, sauté onions and garlic until softened
2. Stir in chickpeas, spinach, coconut milk, curry powder, cumin, paprika, salt, and pepper
3. Simmer for 10-15 minutes, or until spinach is wilted and chickpeas are heated through
4. Serve hot over cooked rice or with naan
5. Enjoy your vegan chickpea and spinach curry!

Substitutions

None

4
servings

320

25

Vegan Lemon
Garlic Pasta

Ingredients:

8 oz pasta
2 cloves garlic (minced)
Zest and juice of 2 lemons
1/4 cup olive oil
2 tbsp fresh parsley (chopped)
Salt and pepper to taste
Red pepper flakes (optional)

Substitutions

None

A simple yet flavorful pasta dish with a zesty lemon and garlic sauce, perfect for a quick weeknight dinner.

Directions

1. Cook pasta according to package instructions
2. In a skillet, heat olive oil and sauté minced garlic until fragrant
3. Stir in lemon zest, lemon juice, salt, and pepper
4. Toss cooked pasta in the lemon garlic sauce
5. Garnish with fresh parsley and red pepper flakes (if desired)
6. Serve hot and enjoy your vegan lemon garlic pasta!

Chapter 10
Quick and Easy Bowls

4
servings

350

30

Vegan Burrito Bowl

A flavor-packed bowl with cilantro-lime rice, black beans, grilled veggies, guacamole, and salsa.

Ingredients:

2 cups cooked brown rice
1 can black beans (drained and rinsed)
2 cups bell peppers (sliced)
1 onion (sliced)
2 cloves garlic (minced)
1 tsp cumin
1 tsp chili powder
Juice of 2 limes
2 avocados (sliced)
1 cup salsa
Fresh cilantro for garnish
Salt and pepper to taste

Directions

1. Cook brown rice according to package instructions
2. In a skillet, sauté onions and garlic until softened
3. Add sliced bell peppers, cumin, chili powder, salt, and pepper
4. Cook until peppers are tender and slightly charred
5. In a separate bowl, mash avocados with lime juice and a pinch of salt to make guacamole
6. Assemble bowls with a base of brown rice, black beans, grilled veggies, guacamole, salsa, and garnish with fresh cilantro
7. Enjoy your vegan burrito bowl!

Substitutions

None

4
servings

280

25

Vegan Soba Noodle Bowl

Ingredients:

8 oz soba noodles
8 oz tofu (cubed)
1 cup edamame (shelled)
2 carrots (julienned)
1 cucumber (sliced)
1/4 cup soy sauce
2 tbsp sesame oil
1 tbsp rice vinegar
1 tbsp maple syrup
1 tsp fresh ginger (grated)
2 cloves garlic (minced)
Sesame seeds for garnish

Substitutions

None

A satisfying noodle bowl with buckwheat soba noodles, tofu, edamame, and a savory sesame ginger sauce.

Directions

1. Cook soba noodles according to package instructions
2. In a skillet, sauté tofu until browned
3. In a large bowl, whisk together soy sauce, sesame oil, rice vinegar, maple syrup, ginger, and garlic to make the sauce
4. Assemble bowls with cooked soba noodles, tofu, edamame, carrots, cucumber, and drizzle with sesame ginger sauce
5. Garnish with sesame seeds
6. Enjoy your vegan soba noodle bowl!

4
servings

320

20

Vegan Mediterranean Bowl

A Mediterranean-inspired bowl with quinoa, falafel, hummus, cucumber, tomato, and a tahini dressing.

Ingredients:

1 cup quinoa
8 falafel balls (store-bought or homemade)
1 cucumber (sliced)
2 tomatoes (chopped)
1/2 cup hummus
1/4 cup tahini
Juice of 1 lemon
2 cloves garlic (minced)
Fresh parsley for garnish
Salt and pepper to taste

Directions

1. Cook quinoa according to package instructions
2. Bake or pan-fry falafel balls according to package instructions
3. In a small bowl, whisk together tahini, lemon juice, minced garlic, salt, and pepper to make the dressing
4. Assemble bowls with cooked quinoa, falafel, cucumber, tomato, and a dollop of hummus
5. Drizzle with tahini dressing and garnish with fresh parsley
6. Enjoy your vegan Mediterranean bowl!

Substitutions

None

4
servings

320

30

Vegan Teriyaki Bowl

Ingredients:

8 oz tofu (cubed)
2 cups broccoli florets
2 carrots (sliced)
1 cup cooked brown rice
1/2 cup teriyaki sauce
2 tbsp vegetable oil
Sesame seeds for garnish
Salt and pepper to taste

Substitutions

None

A delectable bowl with teriyaki-glazed tofu, broccoli, carrots, and brown rice, drizzled with extra teriyaki sauce.

Directions

1. In a skillet, sauté tofu in vegetable oil until browned
2. Pour teriyaki sauce over tofu and cook until glazed
3. In a separate skillet, stir-fry broccoli and carrots until tender
4. Assemble bowls with cooked brown rice, teriyaki-glazed tofu, and stir-fried vegetables
5. Drizzle with extra teriyaki sauce and garnish with sesame seeds
6. Enjoy your vegan teriyaki bowl!

4
servings

350

40

Vegan Bibimbap Bowl

Ingredients:

8 oz tempeh (sliced)
1 cup carrots (julienned)
1 cup spinach
1 cucumber (sliced)
4 cups cooked brown rice
4 eggs (or tofu for vegan option)
4 tbsp gochujang sauce
2 tbsp vegetable oil
Sesame seeds for garnish
Salt and pepper to taste

Substitutions

None

A Korean-inspired bowl with gochujang-marinated tempeh, assorted vegetables, and a fried egg (or tofu for a vegan option).

Directions

1. Marinate tempeh in gochujang sauce for at least 15 minutes
2. In a skillet, cook tempeh until browned
3. In the same skillet, sauté carrots until tender
4. Blanch spinach in boiling water, then drain and season with salt
5. Fry eggs (or tofu) in vegetable oil until whites are set and yolks are still runny
6. Assemble bowls with cooked brown rice, gochujang tempeh, carrots, spinach, cucumber, and top with a fried egg (or tofu)
7. Garnish with sesame seeds
8. Enjoy your vegan bibimbap bowl!

4
servings

380

35

Vegan BBQ Bowl

Ingredients:

2 cans chickpeas (drained and rinsed)
2 sweet potatoes (cubed)
1 cup corn kernels
1/2 cup BBQ sauce
1/4 cup vegan ranch dressing
2 tbsp vegetable oil
Smoked paprika for garnish
Salt and pepper to taste

Substitutions

None

A smoky and savory bowl with BBQ chickpeas, roasted sweet potatoes, corn, and a creamy vegan ranch dressing.

Directions

1. Toss chickpeas in BBQ sauce and roast in the oven until crispy
2. Toss sweet potato cubes in vegetable oil, smoked paprika, salt, and pepper, and roast until tender
3. Assemble bowls with roasted sweet potatoes, BBQ chickpeas, and corn
4. Drizzle with vegan ranch dressing
5. Enjoy your vegan BBQ bowl!

4
servings

320

25

Vegan Taco Bowl

A Tex-Mex-inspired bowl with seasoned lentils, corn, avocado, tomatoes, and a zesty lime-cilantro dressing.

Ingredients:

1 cup dried green or brown lentils
2 cups vegetable broth
1 cup corn kernels
2 avocados (sliced)
2 tomatoes (chopped)
1/4 cup fresh cilantro (chopped)
Juice of 2 limes
2 tbsp olive oil
1 tsp chili powder
1 tsp cumin
Salt and pepper to taste

Directions

1. Rinse lentils and cook in vegetable broth until tender
2. In a bowl, whisk together lime juice, olive oil, chili powder, cumin, salt, and pepper to make the dressing
3. Assemble bowls with cooked lentils, corn, avocado, tomatoes, and drizzle with lime-cilantro dressing
4. Garnish with fresh cilantro
5. Enjoy your vegan taco bowl!

Substitutions

None

4
servings

320

30

Vegan Thai Bowl

A Thai-inspired bowl with coconut rice, red curry tofu, steamed broccoli, and crushed peanuts, drizzled with peanut sauce.

Ingredients:

2 cups jasmine rice
8 oz tofu (cubed)
2 cups broccoli florets
1/2 cup canned coconut milk
2 tbsp red curry paste
1/4 cup peanut sauce
Crushed peanuts and lime wedges for garnish
Salt and pepper to taste

Directions

1. Cook jasmine rice according to package instructions, using coconut milk for extra flavor
2. In a skillet, sauté tofu until browned, then stir in red curry paste
3. Steam broccoli until tender
4. Assemble bowls with coconut rice, red curry tofu, steamed broccoli, and drizzle with peanut sauce
5. Garnish with crushed peanuts and lime wedges
6. Enjoy your vegan Thai bowl!

Substitutions

None

4
servings

280

20

Vegan Breakfast Bowl

Ingredients:

2 cups coconut yogurt
1 cup granola
2 cups mixed berries
1/4 cup maple syrup
Fresh mint leaves for garnish

A wholesome breakfast bowl with creamy coconut yogurt, granola, fresh berries, and a drizzle of maple syrup.

Directions

1. Divide coconut yogurt into bowls
2. Top with granola and mixed berries
3. Drizzle with maple syrup
4. Garnish with fresh mint leaves
5. Enjoy your vegan breakfast bowl!

Substitutions

None

4
servings

350

30

Vegan Power Bowl

A nutrient-packed bowl with quinoa, roasted veggies, avocado, chickpeas, and a tahini dressing.

Ingredients:

1 cup quinoa
2 cups mixed vegetables (e.g., sweet potatoes, broccoli, bell peppers)
2 avocados (sliced)
1 can chickpeas (drained and rinsed)
1/4 cup tahini
Juice of 2 lemons
2 cloves garlic (minced)
Fresh parsley for garnish
Salt and pepper to taste

Directions

1. Cook quinoa according to package instructions
2. Roast mixed vegetables in the oven until tender
3. In a bowl, whisk together tahini, lemon juice, minced garlic, salt, and pepper to make the dressing
4. Assemble bowls with cooked quinoa, roasted veggies, avocado, chickpeas, and drizzle with tahini dressing
5. Garnish with fresh parsley
6. Enjoy your vegan power bowl!

Substitutions

None

Chapter 11
Creative Casseroles

6
servings

350

45

Vegan Shepherd's Pie

A comforting classic with a vegan twist! Layers of savory lentil filling, mashed potatoes, and a golden crust.

Ingredients:

For the Lentil Filling:
1 cup green or brown lentils (cooked)
1 onion (chopped)
2 cloves garlic (minced)
2 carrots (chopped)
1 cup peas (frozen or fresh)
1 can diced tomatoes
2 tbsp tomato paste
2 tsp thyme
2 tsp rosemary
Salt and pepper to taste
For the Mashed Potatoes:
4 cups potatoes (peeled and cubed)
1/2 cup plant-based milk
2 tbsp vegan butter
Salt and pepper to taste

Substitutions

None

Directions

1. Preheat oven to 375°F (190°C)
2. In a large skillet, sauté onions and garlic until fragrant
3. Add carrots and cook until softened
4. Stir in cooked lentils, peas, diced tomatoes, tomato paste, thyme, rosemary, salt, and pepper
5. Simmer for 15-20 minutes, until flavors meld together
6. In a separate pot, boil potatoes until tender
7. Drain and mash with plant-based milk, vegan butter, salt, and pepper
8. In a baking dish, layer the lentil filling, followed by the mashed potatoes
9. Bake for 20-25 minutes, until the top is golden and filling is bubbly
10. Serve your vegan Shepherd's Pie hot
11. Enjoy!

6
servings

320

35

Vegan Mexican Lasagna

Ingredients:

12 corn tortillas
2 cans black beans (drained and rinsed)
2 cups corn (frozen or fresh)
1 red bell pepper (chopped)
1 onion (chopped)
2 cloves garlic (minced)
1 can diced tomatoes
2 tsp chili powder
1 tsp cumin
1 tsp smoked paprika
Salt and pepper to taste
1 cup vegan cheese (optional)
Fresh cilantro for garnish

Substitutions

None

A spicy and layered casserole with corn tortillas, black beans, vegetables, and a smoky chipotle tomato sauce.

Directions

1. Preheat oven to 375°F (190°C)
2. In a skillet, sauté onions and garlic until softened
3. Add chopped red bell pepper, corn, black beans, diced tomatoes, chili powder, cumin, smoked paprika, salt, and pepper
4. Simmer for 10-15 minutes until vegetables are tender
5. In a baking dish, layer corn tortillas, followed by the bean and vegetable mixture, and repeat
6. Top with vegan cheese if desired
7. Bake for 20-25 minutes, until heated through and bubbly
8. Garnish with fresh cilantro
9. Enjoy your vegan Mexican Lasagna!

6
servings

280

40

Vegan Broccoli and Rice Casserole

Ingredients:

2 cups broccoli florets
2 cups cooked brown rice
1 onion (chopped)
2 cloves garlic (minced)
1/4 cup vegan butter
1/4 cup all-purpose flour
2 cups plant-based milk
2 cups vegan cheese (shredded)
Salt and pepper to taste
Nutritional yeast for garnish

Substitutions

None

A creamy and cheesy casserole with broccoli florets, rice, and a dairy-free cheese sauce.

Directions

1. Preheat oven to 375°F (190°C)
2. Steam broccoli florets until tender
3. In a skillet, sauté onions and garlic in vegan butter until softened
4. Stir in flour to create a roux
5. Gradually whisk in plant-based milk until smooth
6. Add 1.5 cups of vegan cheese and continue to whisk until thickened
7. Season with salt and pepper
8. In a baking dish, combine cooked brown rice, steamed broccoli, and the cheese sauce
9. Top with remaining 0.5 cup of vegan cheese and sprinkle with nutritional yeast
10. Bake for 20-25 minutes, until golden and bubbly
11. Enjoy your vegan Broccoli and Rice Casserole!

6
servings

320

30

Vegan Spinach and Artichoke Dip Casserole

A twist on the classic dip! Creamy spinach and artichoke hearts baked with vegan cheese until gooey and irresistible.

Ingredients:

2 cups fresh spinach (chopped)
1 can artichoke hearts (drained and chopped)
1 cup vegan cream cheese
1/2 cup vegan sour cream
1/4 cup vegan mayonnaise
1 cup vegan cheese (shredded)
2 cloves garlic (minced)
Salt and pepper to taste
Vegan parmesan for garnish

Directions

1. Preheat oven to 375°F (190°C)
2. In a skillet, sauté spinach and minced garlic until wilted
3. In a mixing bowl, combine chopped artichoke hearts, vegan cream cheese, vegan sour cream, vegan mayonnaise, and 0.5 cup of vegan cheese
4. Stir in sautéed spinach and garlic
5. Season with salt and pepper
6. Transfer the mixture to a baking dish
7. Top with remaining 0.5 cup of vegan cheese and sprinkle with vegan parmesan
8. Bake for 20-25 minutes until bubbly and golden
9. Enjoy your vegan Spinach and Artichoke Dip Casserole!

Substitutions

None

6
servings

350

50

Vegan Stuffed Cabbage Casserole

Ingredients:

1 small cabbage (shredded)
1 cup green or brown lentils (cooked)
1 cup cooked rice
1 onion (chopped)
2 cloves garlic (minced)
1 can diced tomatoes
2 tbsp tomato paste
2 tsp paprika
1 tsp thyme
1 tsp oregano
Salt and pepper to taste
Fresh parsley for garnish

Substitutions

None

A deconstructed take on stuffed cabbage rolls! Layers of cabbage, lentils, rice, and a rich tomato sauce.

Directions

1. Preheat oven to 375°F (190°C)
2. In a skillet, sauté onions and garlic until fragrant
3. Stir in cooked lentils, cooked rice, diced tomatoes, tomato paste, paprika, thyme, oregano, salt, and pepper
4. Simmer for 10-15 minutes until flavors meld together
5. In a baking dish, layer shredded cabbage, followed by the lentil and rice mixture, and repeat
6. Bake for 25-30 minutes, until cabbage is tender and the top is golden
7. Garnish with fresh parsley
8. Enjoy your vegan Stuffed Cabbage Casserole!

6
servings

380

40

Vegan Enchilada Casserole

Ingredients:

12 corn tortillas
2 cans black beans (drained and rinsed)
2 cups enchilada sauce
1 cup raw cashews (soaked and blended)
1/4 cup nutritional yeast
2 cloves garlic (minced)
1 tsp cumin
1 tsp chili powder
Salt and pepper to taste
Fresh cilantro for garnish

Substitutions

None

A Tex-Mex delight with layers of corn tortillas, black beans, enchilada sauce, and a creamy cashew-based topping.

Directions

1. Preheat oven to 375°F (190°C)
2. In a baking dish, spread a thin layer of enchilada sauce
3. Place 4 corn tortillas on the sauce, followed by half of the black beans
4. Add another layer of enchilada sauce and 4 more tortillas
5. Add the remaining black beans and more enchilada sauce
6. Top with the last 4 tortillas and the rest of the enchilada sauce
7. In a blender, combine soaked cashews, nutritional yeast, minced garlic, cumin, chili powder, salt, and pepper to make the cashew topping
8. Pour the cashew mixture over the casserole
9. Bake for 25-30 minutes, until the top is golden and bubbly
10. Garnish with fresh cilantro
11. Enjoy your vegan Enchilada Casserole!

6
servings

320

45

Vegan Eggplant Parmesan Casserole

Ingredients:

2 large eggplants (sliced)
2 cups breadcrumbs (vegan)
1/2 cup vegan parmesan (grated)
4 cups marinara sauce
2 cups vegan mozzarella (shredded)
2 tsp dried basil
2 tsp dried oregano
Salt and pepper to taste
Fresh basil for garnish

Substitutions

None

A comforting Italian classic with layers of breaded and baked eggplant slices, marinara sauce, and vegan mozzarella.

Directions

1. Preheat oven to 375°F (190°C)
2. Dip eggplant slices in plant-based milk, then coat with a mixture of breadcrumbs, vegan parmesan, dried basil, dried oregano, salt, and pepper
3. Place breaded eggplant slices on a baking sheet and bake for 20-25 minutes until crispy
4. In a baking dish, spread a thin layer of marinara sauce
5. Layer half of the baked eggplant slices on the sauce
6. Top with 2 cups of marinara sauce and 1 cup of vegan mozzarella
7. Repeat with the remaining eggplant, sauce, and mozzarella
8. Bake for 20-25 minutes, until the cheese is melted and bubbly
9. Garnish with fresh basil
10. Enjoy your vegan Eggplant Parmesan Casserole!

6
servings

380

40

Vegan Tater Tot Casserole

Ingredients:

1 bag frozen tater tots
1 package vegan sausage crumbles
2 cups mixed vegetables (e.g., peas, carrots, corn)
1/4 cup vegan butter
1/4 cup all-purpose flour
2 cups plant-based milk
1 cup vegan cheese (shredded)
Salt and pepper to taste
Fresh chives for garnish

Substitutions

None

A nostalgic favorite with layers of crispy tater tots, vegan sausage, veggies, and a creamy dairy-free sauce.

Directions

1. Preheat oven to 375°F (190°C)
2. In a skillet, cook vegan sausage crumbles until browned
3. In a separate pot, melt vegan butter and whisk in flour to create a roux
4. Gradually whisk in plant-based milk until thickened
5. Stir in vegan cheese, salt, and pepper
6. In a baking dish, layer frozen tater tots, cooked sausage crumbles, mixed vegetables, and pour the creamy sauce over the top
7. Bake for 25-30 minutes, until tater tots are golden and the casserole is bubbling
8. Garnish with fresh chives
9. Enjoy your vegan Tater Tot Casserole!

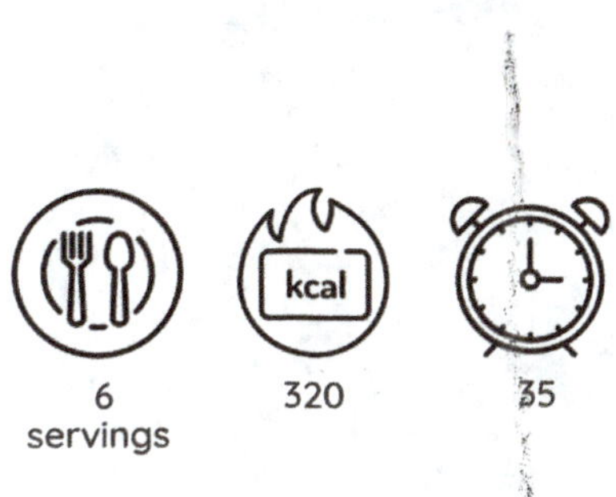

Vegan Sweet Potato and Black Bean Casserole

Ingredients:

3 large sweet potatoes (sliced)
2 cans black beans (drained and rinsed)
4 cups fresh spinach
2 cloves garlic (minced)
1 can diced tomatoes with green chilies
1 tsp chipotle powder
1 tsp cumin
1 tsp smoked paprika
Salt and pepper to taste
Fresh cilantro for garnish

Substitutions

None

A hearty and nutritious casserole with layers of sweet potato, black beans, spinach, and a smoky chipotle sauce.

Directions

1. Preheat oven to 375°F (190°C)
2. In a skillet, sauté minced garlic until fragrant
3. Stir in diced tomatoes with green chilies, chipotle powder, cumin, smoked paprika, salt, and pepper
4. In a baking dish, layer sliced sweet potatoes, black beans, and fresh spinach
5. Pour the tomato mixture over the layers
6. Cover with foil and bake for 30-35 minutes, until sweet potatoes are tender
7. Remove the foil and bake for an additional 10 minutes, until the top is slightly crispy
8. Garnish with fresh cilantro
9. Enjoy your vegan Sweet Potato and Black Bean Casserole!

6
servings

350

50

Vegan Ratatouille Polenta Casserole

A French-inspired delight with layers of ratatouille (vegetable stew) and creamy polenta, baked to perfection.

Ingredients:

For the Ratatouille:
2 cups eggplant (cubed)
2 cups zucchini (sliced)
2 cups bell peppers (sliced)
1 onion (chopped)
2 cloves garlic (minced)
1 can diced tomatoes
2 tsp dried basil
2 tsp dried thyme
Salt and pepper to taste
For the Polenta:
1 cup polenta
4 cups vegetable broth
1/4 cup vegan butter
1/4 cup nutritional yeast
Salt and pepper to taste
Fresh basil for garnish

Substitutions

None

Directions

1. Preheat oven to 375°F (190°C)
2. In a large skillet, sauté onions and garlic until softened
3. Add eggplant, zucchini, bell peppers, diced tomatoes, dried basil, dried thyme, salt, and pepper
4. Simmer for 15-20 minutes until vegetables are tender
5. In a separate pot, bring vegetable broth to a boil
6. Slowly whisk in polenta, stirring constantly
7. Cook polenta according to package instructions, then stir in vegan butter, nutritional yeast, salt, and pepper
8. In a baking dish, layer ratatouille and polenta, starting with ratatouille
9. Bake for 25-30 minutes, until heated through and slightly golden
10. Garnish with fresh basil
11. Enjoy your vegan Ratatouille Polenta Casserole!

We have a small favor to ask

Dear Dedicated Readers,

As we conclude our flavorful journey through the pages of "Plant-Based Diet Made Simple Cookbook: Easy, Delicious, Plant-Based," I want to extend my heartfelt thanks for choosing to embrace the plant-based lifestyle with us. Your dedication to wholesome and compassionate eating is both inspiring and commendable, and for that, we are truly grateful.

This cookbook was crafted with the belief that plant-based eating can be a delicious, accessible, and fulfilling way of nourishing both body and soul. It is our hope that each recipe you've explored within these pages has not only tantalized your taste buds but also offered you a fresh perspective on the vibrant world of plant-based cuisine.

As you reflect on the culinary delights you've discovered here, I would like to make a humble request, one that holds profound significance for us as a small publishing team. Reviews, my dear readers, are the lifeblood of our work.

Your insights and experiences, expressed through reviews, have the power to inspire, inform, and guide fellow food enthusiasts in their plant-based journeys. By sharing your thoughts with the world, you become a vital part of a community that is striving to make the world a healthier and more sustainable place, one meal at a time.

If the recipes and ideas within this cookbook have contributed to your culinary adventures and enriched your everyday meals, we kindly ask that you take a moment to support us by leaving a review. A simple star rating and a brief sentence or two on the platform or app where you acquired this cookbook can have a profound impact.

Your review is not just a review; it's a gesture of support and encouragement to others who are considering embracing plant-based eating. It's a valuable testament to the transformative power of the food we choose to put on our plates.

Reviews, whether they praise our work or offer constructive feedback, hold a special place in our hearts. They are the compass that guides us in our ongoing mission to provide you with culinary resources that cater to your tastes and values.

While we have poured our hearts and souls into creating this cookbook, it's essential to acknowledge that, as in all human endeavors, imperfections can occasionally surface. Your feedback is the bridge that helps us to refine our craft, learn, and grow.

In the spirit of fostering a more inclusive, compassionate, and sustainable world through food, I would like to express my deepest gratitude for your support of "Plant-Based Diet Made Simple." Your feedback and engagement help us connect with readers from diverse walks of life and bring us one step closer to our vision of a healthier planet.

Thank you for entrusting us to be part of your culinary journey. Your support means the world to us, and we look forward to continuing our shared exploration of the plant-based culinary landscape.